THE LIFE OF LITTLE GEORGE HENDERSON

First edition. February 10, 2023.

Copyright © 2023 Jennifer D. Anger-Baeta.

ISBN: 979-8215769287

Written by Jennifer D. Anger-Baeta.

This book is dedicated to the hundreds of unknown infants and children that lie in unmarked graves within the Citizens Cemetery in Prescott, Arizona, and to the pioneer families that loved those children.

And to my mother and father, for teaching me how to follow my dreams.

The Life of Little George Henderson

Pioneer Tales from Yavapai County, Arizona

Jennifer D. Anger-Baeta

Based on a true story.

Chapter 1

February 2020 - Dewey, Arizona

It was a hectic morning, and the phone had not stopped ringing. Jennifer moved swiftly across the small room and clumsily dropped a thick stack of files onto her desk and then answered another incoming call. She took a quick breath, pushed down a growing sense of frustration, made a conscious effort to smile, and then placed the phone to her ear as she said, "good afternoon. How can I help you?"

"Hey, I recognize that fake chipper tone. It means that you must be pretty busy today. I hate to do this to you, but I have a problem on the job site, and I could use your help." Jennifer recognized the voice on the other end of the line. She knew that he usually did not call unless something had gone wrong. She asked inquisitively, "what do you mean? What is going on with the job site?"

Jennifer heard Mark let out an anxious sigh as he began to explain, "well, I am in the excavator, and I was digging in this washed-out area on this residential job site in our neighborhood and I thought that there was something unusual in the material. I actually had to stop working because I found a headstone and it is currently hanging from my bucket."

Jennifer gasped in surprise and then quickly asked, "what? are you serious? That can't be! That is a residential site, and there is not supposed to be a gravesite anywhere near there. Are you certain that what you have found is actually a headstone?"

Mark heard the shock and the surprise in Jennifer's voice, and he began to laugh as he replied, "that was my reaction too. But, as sure as I am sitting here talking to you, there is a headstone hanging from my bucket. Unfortunately, I am probably going to have to shut down the job site. I can't risk digging on a gravesite, and I need a little help figuring out what I am supposed to do next here."

Jennifer took a deep breath and thought for a moment about what needed to happen, and then she said, "I hate to say it, but I think that you're right, and if there is a gravesite on that residential property, then you are going to have to shut the job down, and you are also going to need to call the Yavapai County sheriff's department to report the finding."

Jennifer paused for the briefest moment before asking, "would you mind giving me the name and the dates that are on the headstone?"

Mark let out a quick sigh and then said, "not at all. Sure. But I don't know what the headstone says yet because I'm still sitting in the cab of my machine, and I'm just staring at this thing that is hanging from my bucket. I guess the next thing that I need to do is to figure out what the engraving says. Let me get out and take a better look at it, and then I will call the Sheriff's department. Let me get those things done and then I'll call you back."

"Yeah, that all sounds good. I'll get the computer going so that I can do some research since it sounds like you are going to need it. By the way, if you can do it and if you wouldn't mind, can you send me a photo of the headstone please?" Jennifer asked politely as she eagerly snapped her laptop open and perched it on her desk beside the stack of files as Mark pressed the end call button on his cell phone. Jennifer placed her phone down carefully beside the computer. It only took a few seconds for the phone to chime as it received a text message with a photo of the headstone.

Jennifer sat down, suddenly becoming aware of how hard and uncomfortable the wooden seats in the dark basement office were. She let out a sigh, shuffled in her seat and attempted to make the best of her comfort, and then cautiously unlocked the phone's screen. The image of the headstone popped up on the screen, and Jennifer let out a short and sharp gasp at the sight of the image. She stared intensely at the image as she evaluated the perfectly rounded top and the decorative engraved leafing. Everything about the stone was perfect. It was exquisite.

Jennifer was captivated by the image. She spent several minutes evaluating the headstone, and placed her finger over the screen and was delicately tracing the names and the dates that were engraved on the face of the stone when the screen was suddenly interrupted by an incoming call. Jennifer was startled by the call, but she shrugged and then quickly tapped on the accept call icon, and then on the speakerphone icon and asked, "Mark, how is it going? Did you manage to get into contact with someone down at the sheriff's department?"

There was a brief moment of silence and then the voice on the other end of the line spoke calmly and slowly, "yeah, I did. The officer that I talked to said that he is going to send someone out to take a look around. He confirmed that I should stop working for now until someone can figure out where the grave is located. Unfortunately, it does not sound like this visit is going to provide me with a fast fix because the officer couldn't find any permits or any records for any gravesites on this property. Basically, there is not supposed to be a gravesite here, and nobody seems to know exactly where the body is."

Jennifer could hear the tension rising in Mark's voice as he spoke, and she scrunched up her face as she replied, "it certainly is very odd. Well, I am not certain that there is anything that I can do to be helpful, but I can try to research it and I can at least try to figure out where the remains are. I mean, I hate to sound morbid, but you know as well as anybody else does that where there is a headstone, there is usually a body. And, where there is a body, there is usually some form of documentation that explains what took place, like permits. Let me at least give it a shot and I will see what I can come up with, and then I'll call you back."

Her fingers were already tapping away at the keyboard on the laptop computer that was in front of her before Mark could reply. Mark took a second to think about the suggestion, and though he was doubtful that her research would provide any results, he eventually agreed. He tried to mask the doubt in his tone when he replied, "that would be great. It's hard enough thinking about dealing with a stop-work order, but now I have this worry that I have been digging on a gravesite. Whatever you can find on it, give me a call back and let me know."

Jennifer autonomously tapped on the phone screen to end the call. Her full focus shifted to what was displayed on the computer screen in front of her.

The time went by quickly, and Jennifer was so consumed with the research that she was conducting that she was unaware that several hours had passed when the phone began to ring. She looked at the display showing the incoming call and the clock beside it, and then took a deep breath and answered the call by stating apologetically, "Mark, I am so glad that you called. I'm really sorry that I didn't call you back. I know that it has been a while since we spoke earlier, but I needed some time to verify some of the information that I found, and I think that I have some pretty great news for you."

"You do?" Mark's voice sounded genuinely nervous as he continued, "that's great, because right now I have a Yavapai County Sheriff's officer here on the job site, and he is still saying that nobody can find any of the records for the gravesite. He also said that he is going to have to request that the county give us a stop-work order until they can research it further and they can figure out exactly where the gravesite is. This is just not what I needed to have happen. A stop-work order like this one could take months to resolve. I have to stay on schedule, and I really just don't have time for a stop-work order right now, you know?"

"Oh my gosh! Well, it is a good thing that I know where the gravesite is then. If the sheriff is there now, can you please ask him to stay there? I can jump in my car, and I can be there in a couple of minutes. I am already walking out to my car as I speak. I'll see you in a few." Jennifer rushed to grab her car keys and her purse and then hurried out to her car.

"Yeah, he is still here. I can ask him to wait for you. Not a problem. Just be careful." Mark pressed the end call button and looked back towards the sheriff that was inspecting the property in the area where the headstone was found. He watched as the officer inspected the ground and the dirt in the washed-out area in much the same fashion that Mark himself had done. The officer's eyes darted from behind dark sunglasses as he scanned and surveyed the landscape, attempting to assess what might have happened, looking for any sign of any clue that might explain where the gravesite was.

The officer continued to scan the dirt and scrutinized the earth around him and then stated suddenly, "you know, this is the only call that I have ever received like this. I have lived here all of my life, and I have been with the sheriff's office for more than 20 years, and I have never received a call where someone found a gravesite or a headstone out here. Nobody down at the station that I've talked to has ever heard of anything like this happening in this area before either."

Mark brushed his hand through his short blonde hair and smirked as he shifted his focus and looked down towards the area where he had located the headstone, and then said, "that's probably not such a bad thing."

Only a few moments passed by when both Mark and the officer heard Jennifer's car approaching from the north side of the property from the dirt road. They both turned to watch the black vehicle as it slowly turned in and stopped in the driveway, and then they casually walked towards the driveway.

Jennifer stopped the car and rushed to exit the vehicle. She was so excited by what she had discovered that she was already shouting and beginning to explain what she had found to the officer before she could completely exit the vehicle. "Oh my goodness, this headstone is shocking, and I can't believe those dates! The information about the family is incredibly interesting!"

Jennifer smiled brightly as she quickly and cautiously closed the door to her car. She glanced at Mark and then turned towards the approaching officer. She took a quick breath, and then stated warmly, "I am sorry. It seems that I am getting ahead of myself, please forgive me. My name is Jennifer. It's a pleasure to meet you, Officer. Sir." Jennifer extended her hand to the officer as she spoke.

The officer smiled at Jennifer's unusual mannerisms and extended his hand back to her. As they shook hands he stated his name, "I am Officer Mason with the Yavapai County Sheriff's Department. It's nice to meet you, Ma'am."

Jennifer took a quick breath, looked up at the officer, and stated confidently, "Sir, finding the headstone is a surprise because there isn't supposed to be a gravesite out here on a residential property. But I believe that I have collected enough evidence that I can prove what happened here."

The officer was amused by her statement, and he quickly took notice of her long, wild, amber-colored hair, her small frame, and her soft hazel eyes. He smiled with a raised eyebrow, focused on the case, and said, "okay. Then, humor me."

Jennifer looked up at the tall, dark-haired officer, and she smiled gently at him as she began to explain, "the headstone is for a George Graham Henderson, Jr., born on December 15th, 1890. The headstone is more than 120 years old and the history behind it goes a long way back. It is shocking to have found the headstone in a rural and residential location like this, but what is even more unusual is how many things went wrong right here on this property that ultimately caused his death."

Chapter 2
December 14th, 1890 - Quebec, Canada

Melissa stood in her living room in front of a small picture-frame window and watched as the wind whipped the tops of the tall white birch trees that lined their farm. The snow had begun to flurry, and there was a drift forming from the northeast corner of the roof, creating growing hills of soft, powdery white snow. Melissa had just taken notice of the collecting snow on the ground below when she heard a strange and unfamiliar noise and then felt a sudden rush of fluid that ran down her slender, alabaster legs.

"George! George!" Melissa shrieked in panic. She knew what this meant. Her water had broken, and it was time. The baby was coming.

George was chopping firewood in his small, drafty workshop when he heard Melissa's screams coming from within the house. The distressed shrieking sound in her voice had put him in such a hurry to get back inside of the house that he bounded across the snowy yard, and then he forgot to shake off the snow from his clothing and his boots as he rushed into the house to help her. George was startled by the noise, but he was relieved when he found Melissa standing in front of the living room window where she was cradling her bulging belly.

George quickly closed the door behind him and then stood in front of the doorway and watched his wife curiously for a moment, and as he started to recognize the meaning behind the expression that was on her face he asked almost sheepishly, "is it time? Is it really time?"

Melissa looked at her husband and shook her head frantically while she exclaimed, "yes, it is! I know that it's about three weeks early, but my water just broke!"

Though he was still in his outdoor winter clothes, George moved cautiously towards his wife. He stopped and stood in front of her, looked down at her beautiful face and smiled as he gracefully wrapped his arms around her and carefully lifted her off of her feet. Her arms draped around his neck softly as he lifted her and carried her across the small living room and into the bedroom where they were already prepared to deliver the baby.

George did everything that he could to make Melissa feel comfortable before leaving her for only a few minutes in order to call on the midwife. It was a brief absence, and Melissa was relieved when George returned with her neighbor, her midwife, and her friend, Helena. Helena was several years older than Melissa, but despite their age difference, they were very close and had become the best of friends over the years.

Having both George and Helena by her side, Melissa was as comfortable as she could be. As time went on, Melissa's labor became increasingly more difficult, and she struggled to find the energy and the strength that she needed to endure the slow, hard labor. George and Helena encouraged Melissa to breathe through each intense wave of physical pain, and with every painful contraction, she became more and more exhausted.

After nearly twenty hours of hard labor, George emerged from his and Melissa's bedroom and sat down in front of the fireplace beside their four children, Robert, William, Harry, and Pearl. The children were still too young to notice from the appearance of their father's eyes that he had been crying. George wiped the tears and the perspiration from his face onto a handkerchief, took a long breath, and then spoke slowly as his young children looked up at him.

"Your mother had a really difficult time with," George let his voice and his words trail off into thin air as he looked down at the four sets of innocent eyes staring back at him.

He took a jagged and raspy breath and tried to explain it again, "your mother is very tired, but you can come into the bedroom with me to see her in just a minute. Before I take you in there though, I need to explain a few things to you. The baby was breech, which basically means that the baby was turned in a bad position. It was a very scary situation, and your mother had a very difficult time with the delivery.

Fortunately the midwife Helena, she knew what to do, and everything turned out alright. Your mother has given you a new baby brother, and we've already decided that we want to name him George Graham Henderson, Jr."

The baby was perfect. But the winter had been hard on both George and Melissa, and her pregnancy had not been easy. As the winter set in, and the temperatures became colder and the snowdrifts grew larger, Melissa complained about the cold conditions more frequently than she had in the years before. During the last trimester of her pregnancy she frequently complained that she felt generally unwell, and often said that she was suffering from unusual headaches that seemed to become more severe in the cold, wintry temperatures.

George looked at his children that were wrapped in thick blankets as they sat in front of the warm fireplace, and the scene was a stark reminder that he was forced to work a lot harder in the icy cold temperatures in order to guarantee that his family would be kept safe and warm. It had become increasingly harder to provide for his family's comfort as he aged and as his family grew. For years, both George and Melissa had been sharing their dreams of living in warmer weather, particularly during the long, frigid winters.

George pushed down the thought, smiled brightly as he looked down at his children, and said, "you're going to have to try to keep yourselves calm. But if you can do that, then you can come back into the other room to meet your new little baby brother."

The children rushed to their feet and scrambled to get into the bedroom to see their mother and the new baby. The children burst into the bedroom, and they were so excited to see the baby that it sent both Melissa and George into a fit of laughter.

Melissa looked at her children's young faces and then gently turned the baby around in her arms so that they would all be able to see his face clearly, and asked, "what do you think of him? He's a cute little guy, isn't he?"

Pearl looked at her little brother and said excitedly, "baby Georgie. He's so cute! But Mama, why is it so cold in here? Shouldn't you bring the baby into the other room and keep him by the fire where he can stay warm?"

George walked over to the children that had all lined themselves up at the side of their mother's bed, and then placed his hand on his daughter's shoulder, looked down at her, and smiled. As he turned to look towards his wife, he said, "Pearl is right, Liz. It is quite cold in here. Maybe when you're ready to get up you can bring the baby into the main room where it's warmer."

Melissa shook and bobbed her head as she replied, "I know that it is cold in here, but I have him bundled up and he is staying warm. If you think that it's cold in here, you should go and take a look at the snow that's on the ground outside."

George looked across the room and out of a small window and gazed over the landscaping that was covered by billows of powdery snow. He smiled weakly, and then gently reminded her, "yeah, I saw it. I was out chopping firewood in the snow yesterday when your water broke and this whole having the baby stuff started. But, Liz, the snow, and this cold weather, it is really starting to get to me. It is very cold outside, and it is incredibly cold in here. Every winter presents us with the challenge to keep the house warm enough for our safety, and I'm afraid that I can't keep up with it as well as I used to. There are places that we could go where it would be a lot warmer and a lot less daunting during the winter. I know that you probably don't want to talk about it right now but, there are a lot of opportunities for ranchers and miners in the southern United States."

Melissa looked up at George, gave him a thin smile, tilted her head, and said, "oh, are you going to start on that again? I have only just given birth to this little angel, and you practically have us on the train to Mexico already."

Melissa looked down at the baby boy that she was holding in her arms and smiled. She always spoke her mind, and it was one of the things that George loved about her the most. She was a strikingly beautiful woman, with long, shiny brown hair, and mesmerizing green eyes. However beautiful he thought that she was, it was her sharp wit and her clever nature that George actually admired the most.

George let out a soft chuckle, and said, "no, not Mexico exactly. Mexico is in the south, but we won't need to go nearly that far. Lately I have been giving quite a lot of thought to the opportunities that are out there in Arizona."

"Arizona? George, you know that I love you. Right? But Arizona is not a part of the federal United States yet, and it is a territory that belonged to Mexico until just a few years ago. And aren't those people still fighting each other over the territory? They can't even agree on what to call the place, Mexico, New Mexico, or Arizona. I mean, I have read the newspapers and it is pretty clear based on the news reports that the people in that region can't agree on anything. How is that supposed to be better for us than it is here? Not to mention that it is a real desert that far south, and I don't even know what it is like to be in the desert. Sure, the winters will be warmer, but how much hotter will the summers be? The desert is very different from what we are used to, but is the desert the right kind of different?" Melissa was not truly against the idea, though George knew from what he heard in her tone that she was reluctant.

George looked at his wife excitedly and asked, "Liz, isn't that what we have been talking about? Isn't that what you said that you wanted for the kids? This could be very beneficial for all of us. Life is supposed to be about the adventure and getting out there and experiencing what it's like to live somewhere else. Just think of the warmer winters. You're probably right about the high temperatures in the summer, but there are ways of dealing with that. If we are nearby a lake, it means more fun and more enjoyment during the summer. But most importantly, it will mean that we will have more opportunities for our family and for our farm. Arizona has been in the news for years because of the gold. Every newspaper and every telegraph tells it like it is. Arizona is full of cowboys, miners, and gold. There is supposedly Cortez gold, and Aztec gold, and gold-gold."

George was more amused by his double use of the word gold than Melissa was. Melissa looked down at the newborn baby that she was holding in her arms while she listened to her husband ramble on.

George looked eagerly at his wife, smiled, and then continued, "you know, baby, I work hard as a farmer and a rancher so that you and the kids will always have everything that you need. And the work that I have been doing on the roads for the city gives us a little extra money but, it comes at a big cost, you know. I am not getting any younger, and every year it gets a little more painful and a little harder to get everything done. Don't get me wrong, I will give every season everything that I have got for you and the kids. But I'm getting old, Liz, and I don't know how many more years of working like this that I have got in me."

Melissa looked up at George's face and she smiled tenderly. George's once youthful face was now more lined and more mature. His dark hair was showing its first signals of gray. Though they were both growing older, she still loved everything about the man that she saw standing in front of her.

Melissa knew that George was right. She also noticed all of the changes that had occurred throughout the years. Every year it was becoming a little more difficult to keep the children warm, and every year it was more difficult to keep them healthy. Every year was more daunting and more challenging than the years before.

George continued, "just think, baby. We can pack up everything that we want to take with us, we can sell what we can't take, and then we can just go. We can take the kids and find a little house, maybe near some water in the country, or up in the mountains somewhere, and maybe we might even find a little gold."

Melissa interrupted George from going on any further by asking, "and what if we do move there, and what if you never find any gold? Then what? I know that the newspapers are reporting about the cases where some lucky miner found a large quantity of gold. But how many miners have gone there with their hopes and their big dreams of finding gold, only to find a life of challenging work and disappointment? It is a lot of promise of gold. But what if the other news is what is true, and what if all that is in Arizona is cowboys, Indians, diseases, and frontier mayhem?"

George laughed heartily, and as he attempted to settle himself back down, he asked with a giggle, "Melissa, what exactly is frontier mayhem?"

He could not help but to chuckle again at his wife's suggestion. George had read many of the newspapers that were printed in the southwestern region, and he knew that there were real problems that existed in the world. There was famine, drought, and disease. There were reports that described the occasional problems that occurred with the native or indigenous populations, and there were reports that covered the occasional incidents involving seemingly random violence. However, George had been studying the region for some time and he concluded that most of these occurrences involving violence were usually targeted events, and the indigenous people and the new European settlers were getting along quite well in reality.

George recalled a specific article that was published in the newspaper which explained that the indigenous or native populations in the southwestern region actually considered the new settlers to be their white brothers and sisters. George knew that the news that he had read about Arizona was not significantly different from the news that came out about any other place. In reality, the world was filled with small communities that were made up of good-natured, hard-working, and decent people, and there were genuine opportunities to be had in the southwest.

Melissa rolled her eyes and stated flatly, "you're laughing at me when my concerns are genuine."

George smiled brightly and couldn't resist letting out another little chuckle as he replied, "Liz, you know how the world really works, and you know a lot about business. The news that we get is designed to highlight the most extreme situations whether they are evil or good natured. The media uses the shock and awe factor to create value, because that is what sells their paper."

Melissa quietly nodded her head in agreement.

George continued, "as it pertains to gold, the truth is that we might not find any gold. But I am a rancher and a blacksmith, and I've had a little luck in politics here. I can fall back on any or all of those professions there. As I have already said, Arizona is for farmers and miners. In reality, I might not find any gold. But it can't be any worse living there than it is living here."

Melissa pulled her hand away from her new baby to gently poke and tickle her husband in the side and stated playfully, "but that is my concern. What if it is not as good there as it is here? Maybe all that is there are cowboys and cows."

George replied with a tone that was a little more serious than was necessary, "it's not. It's hard-working people and opportunity."

George recognized his defensive tone, and he took the next opportunity to gently slide his wife's hand into his own and said softly, "just think about it for a while. Imagine having the opportunity to get out of this giant snowball. We could spend a few years down there in the southern sunshine, and if you decide that you don't like it, we can always move west from there, maybe to some town near the ocean in Southern California. Who knows, maybe things will work out and we will spend our whole lives together in Arizona, and it winds up being where I live out the last of my days."

Melissa smiled, looked up at her husband and replied softly, "I promise to think about it."

Chapter 3
April 1892 - Quebec, Canada

Melissa looked back over her shoulder one last time. The coolness in the early spring air felt fresh on her face as she stood in still motion with one hand perched on the railing, and her dark purple dress pulled over to the side in order to allow her legs to safely pass one another on the climb up the stairs and into the train car. She knew that the moment had been coming, and it was finally here. It was her final chance to take one last look at the city that she had always called home.

It was the only home that she had ever known, and it was the place that she associated with all of her fondest memories and the most important moments of her life. It was the place where she had been raised, where she had married her husband, and it was where she was already happily raising her children. She took one last look at the tall white birch trees and the colorful pink cherry trees, took a deep breath, closed her eyes, tried not to think about her parents or the lifetime of friends that she was leaving behind, and turned to quickly climb up the steps into the train car.

After ensuring that the luggage and the children were all safely on board, George held out his hand to his wife to assist her in boarding the train. Melissa grabbed George's hand and looked up at her husband with tears and apprehension in her eyes.

"Liz. It will be okay, baby. Come on. We have a big private sleeper cabin that should have a couple of beds and enough space to be comfortable enough to relax and get some rest. It should be right this way." George nodded and looked towards the front of the train car, recognizing the direction that they needed to take to get to their cabin.

Melissa pushed down the raw emotions, swooped little George up into her arms, and had the toddler quickly seated on her hip. The other children followed in their father's footsteps and into the cabin, where they quickly took a liking to everything that they could reach and put their hands on. Melissa followed and entered the cabin last with little

George seated on her hip. She slid the glass cabin door closed behind them, and then placed little George on a seat beside his siblings.

Melissa yawned as she looked down at George who was already seated, and then asked, "George, I am already exhausted. Is there any possibility that we can speed this trip up and arrive there a little sooner?" As she spoke, she looked around at the small train cabin and observed the neatly made beds. She smiled at the children playing happily in their seats, and then moved towards the empty seat beside her husband and collapsed into it.

George smiled and said, "I know. It's exhausting. I am already feeling the weight of the trip on my shoulders too. But we have a couple of beds, and we can sleep here, and we will stay in some hotels along the way where you will get a hot meal and you can take a long, hot bath, and get recharged for the next train ride. And we do that for a few weeks." George spoke the last sentence fast, and he put on his biggest smile in an attempt to mask the misery that they both expected to experience during the three-week trip.

Melissa leaned over in her seat so that her cheek was resting against George's shoulder, and then she said sadly, "I know. This is the part of the trip that I have been looking forward to the least. The leaving part. Everything that I know is here, and I am leaving almost everything that I have ever loved, including my parents, to sit on a train for a month."

"Three weeks." George interjected.

"On a train," Melissa objected and then paused deliberately before continuing, "for three weeks, which is almost a month. Not to mention that you need to factor in that this trip has a relatively unknown destination. Don't get me wrong, Arizona sounds like it is going to be a great place to live. Finally, no more of those long, ice-cold winters. Still, without ever having seen it, I honestly don't know what to expect, and all I can do is just hope that the decision to move south turns out to be as good as it sounds."

Melissa leaned further into George's shoulder, and as she watched the children playing quietly, she let out a long sigh, and smiled. She was far more tired than she was willing to admit to her husband. She had spent a lot of time worrying about the move, and she was particularly concerned about moving to the unfamiliar territory with the children because of the impact that it might have on them and their future.

George replied calmly, "I know that you have your concerns about all of this. But I truly believe that this move is going to lead us to the types of opportunities that will provide us with the kind of life that we want to build for our family." George leaned his head over and felt his wife's silky hair against his cheek as he placed a gentle kiss on her forehead.

Melissa took a deep breath and pouted, "well, I hope that you're right. After all, we are leaving our entire lives behind. We are leaving everyone that we love, and everything that we have ever known, everything that is comfortable and familiar."

George looked sideways towards his wife, noticed that her eyes were beginning to flood with tears, and then said, "look at how excited the kids are about this move, Liz. William and Harry have been planning for their new bedroom, and they have some pretty lofty ideas about how they want to paint and decorate it. Pearl keeps going on and on about how excited she is that she is going to get to take care of the livestock and the animals that we are planning to get. And Little Georgie has been carrying around a toy train for weeks, and he hasn't stopped talking about how his train is going to Arizona."

Melissa scoffed, gently rolled her teary eyes, and interrupted, "he's just been repeating you."

George laughed and replied, "maybe a little bit. But that excitement is all his own. It is a big move, and I know that it's scary. But as long as we are all together, everything is going to turn out okay."

Melissa smiled warmly, blinked back at the tears that were welling up in her eyes, and said, "I know, and you're right. I love you, George."

In reply, her husband, and her little boy, both looked at her and said, "I love you, too."

Chapter 4
May 1892 – Arizona

After three weeks and two days, Melissa and George eagerly watched the landscape as it passed by the large window of their train car. April had quickly turned into May, and Melissa was delighted by the earliest of the desert blooms that were making their first appearances for the season. She was awe-stricken by the delicate flowers that grew from the smallest of crevices along the mountains and the boulders as they crossed through the last distance of the expansive desert and into the impressive Granite Dells. She was genuinely amused by the foliage and the wide variety of colorful, wiry shrubs.

Melissa's eyes widened as she gazed across the vast landscape. The beauty of the terrain in all of its forms overtook her for a moment as she scrutinized the expansive field of mountains in the background behind the giant jutting rocks. Melissa turned to smile brightly at her husband and then stated excitedly, "George, I believe that this is the strangest and the most beautiful place that I have ever seen! The rocks look like they are growing out of the earth just like the trees around them. Some of them are taller than the pine trees. And the Pines- I had no idea that there would be so many pine trees! It looks like a real forest. I had no idea that it would look like this. It is absolutely breathtaking."

George took a quick but deep breath and replied with a satisfied smile, "I am very relieved to hear you say that."

Melissa was nearly in tears over the sight of the giant granite boulders as she exclaimed, "look, everyone! Look at how wild everything is! Look at the giant rocks and look at how those giant pine trees are growing out of the smallest, tiniest little cracks, and crevices in between them! Look!"

Certainly, Melissa could not wait to get off of the train, and as far as she was concerned, she would be happy if she never had to get on another train again. But, at that moment, she was consumed with what she was seeing, and she was energized by something different, something much deeper and much more meaningful. This new place, this wild, beautiful terrain with its towering pine trees, its jutting rocks, and majestic mountains, this was where they were going to settle down and where they were going to raise their family.

The image of what the future might look like flooded Melissa's vision. She saw a cute little white house with green painted trim and a white picket fence. She envisioned the back of the house, and it was flowing with rows of mature fruit-bearing trees, where every spring the blossoms would fill the air with the sweet fragrance of plums, apples, and pears. Melissa could see the children in her mind, and she watched them as they played, running around the trees. She could see little George swinging on a knotted rope that was hanging from one of the strongest branches in an apple tree while the older children ran around the young boy. The children were smiling and laughing loudly as they played in the fresh, warm spring air.

In her vision, she could hear the noise coming from a horse that was slowly approaching the front of the house, and she turned just in time to see George riding home after a long, hard day of work. His bright blue eyes and his flashy smile broadened as he jumped off of the horse and he hurriedly tied it to a hitching post along the front fence. George turned and then reached into both of his front trouser pockets, and Melissa could have sworn that the sunshine glinted gold on George's front teeth as he smiled, and his hands came out of his pockets with two handful-sized gold nuggets.

Melissa was startled and abruptly snapped back to reality by the sound of George's voice. "Alright, it is time to start getting ready for the train to arrive. We are almost there. I think our stop is just another ten minutes away, and we want to be able to get off of the train quickly and without anything falling off, breaking, or without any other damage. And you all need to watch out for your little brother."

"Oh," Melissa interjected. "Don't worry about him too much. I will have little Georgie with me. I can carry him, and I don't mind it so much while he is still small. He is already growing up too fast, and it won't be long before he will be too grown up, and then I will not be able to carry him anymore." Melissa was happy to carry the children around as long as she could. In Melissa's estimation, holding onto the children as long as she could while they were small was important. She had already experienced it with their older children, and she already knew that the youngest children would outgrow the carrying, the co-sleeping, and the holding onto one another, all too soon.

George and Melissa began arranging the small bags that were on board with them. Melissa focused her attention on their luggage tickets and ensured that they were organized so that George could quickly retrieve the boxes that were filled with the few personal belongings that they brought along with them on the long journey. Most of the contents were clothing and toys that belonged to the children. There were also a few cups and plates that Melissa had acquired from her grandmother that she was not willing to part with, and a few family photos that were considered special. George and Melissa's family members had posed for a minimum of 20 minutes to capture the moments in photographic prints, and not only was it time-consuming, but it had also been an expensive process. Their possessions did not have any real financial or monetary value, but, to George and Melissa, the contents of the small boxes meant absolutely everything.

The sudden sound of screeching erupted from underneath the train car. George looked at the children sprawled lazily across the seats of the cabin and announced, "that is it, kids. That sound means that the train is braking, and we will be pulling into the train station in a few minutes. Remember to wait for the train to come to a complete stop at the station before you start getting up onto your feet. Okay?"

The children began to talk and babble excitedly over one another. George smiled and looked over at Melissa to find her looking and smiling tenderly back at him. The two reached out and placed their hands together and interlaced their fingers as the train came to a slow and gentle stop.

As soon as the train came to a complete stop, Melissa was the first to jump up and onto her feet. George chuckled to himself as it occurred to him that he had never seen Melissa move so fast. She was up and standing, and she swooped up little George and had him positioned on her hip in a matter of seconds. There she stood with her green eyes glowing, looking down at George who was still in his seat, and with a crooked and excited smile she asked, "what are you waiting for, lazybones? We're finally here. We made it. So, let's go!"

Melissa did not waste a moment, and she was already on the move. She had the door to the train cabin open before George could even get to his feet. She could not get out of the cabin fast enough. She hurried down the short hall and rushed by the conductor of the train car and turned in a hurry to exit through the first available door. With little George on her hip, she cautiously pulled the skirt of her long pale blue dress to the side and took the steps down from the train car and stepped down onto the platform carefully, and then she looked up to greet the city that was standing in front of her.

Melissa had read the newspapers, and she had heard the stories from her husband, but for months she had been uncertain of what she should have expected from the new place. As Melissa stood on the platform and looked around at the city of Prescott, for the first time, the scenery took her breath away.

The city was far more modern than she had imagined that it would be. There were electrical poles strung with electrical lines, and rows of electric automobiles parked next to a row of horses along the side of the road. The architecture was drastically different from what she had envisioned of the region, considering that it was the west. Melissa had expected smaller wooden structures and more dilapidated conditions. Instead, there were rows of tall buildings, with bustling businesses, hotels, apartments, restaurants, bars, hardware stores, and churches.

Melissa was impressed by the new city, and she quickly decided that it was as modern as it was wild and beautiful. Melissa looked to both the west and the east of the platform and beyond the downtown area, and she immediately admired the bungalows and the pretty little farmhouses that lined the nearby roads. Houses with white picket fences.

George stepped off of the train car with his children following closely behind him. The children all carefully stepped down from the train, and then stood quietly beside their mother and their father as they all took in the new sights within their new surroundings.

George adjusted his vest and his coat, then smiled at Melissa's wide-eyed stare, and said, "Liz, the children are pretty tired. I think I should try to get us a carriage that can take us to the hotel. It will be easier to move the boxes and the kids if we get some help. Then we will only spend a few days in the hotel, and during that time we can find a nice little house to move into."

Melissa smiled brightly at George and the idea. Her green eyes sparkled as she replied, "that sounds like a great plan! You get the carriage. I'll keep track of the kids."

George spun on his heel, turning to search for a carriage, and then walked away while exclaiming with a brilliant smile, "Liz, I'm going to do it!"

Chapter 5
July 1893 - Walker, Arizona

The intense summer sun was bearing down on the little house that George bought for his family just outside of Prescott, in a little town called Walker. Melissa decided that adapting to the new summer climate was mostly exhausting. There had been a swatch of storms that had moved through the area the week before, and Melissa found that the monsoon storms provided a reprieve from the unbearable summer heat. Still, while the recent rains had cooled the temperatures and elevated the creeks and rivers, it was doing truly little to improve the weather for Melissa on that hot, dry summer day.

Melissa was struggling. She was miserably uncomfortable, and the heat of the summer made her contractions all the more difficult to endure. She had already been laboring for hours, and in the dreaded heat, it felt like an eternity had already passed.

"I have to get up. I cannot just lay here sweating through this pain anymore. I have to get up and walk around." Melissa stammered in frustration as George helped her to get up and into a standing position.

"Okay, baby. Stay steady on your feet, Liz." George was nervous about his wife walking around while she was laboring with his child. Several times the contractions had come on so hard that it had brought Melissa to her knees, and George had to assist her with getting back up onto her feet. He wanted to pick her up and carry her into the bedroom, but as he looked at her and considered the strain that had been put on his back since they first arrived in Arizona, he knew that she was going to have to carry her own weight this time. It was a shocking moment that revealed a stark reality. It was the first moment that George felt truly old. He was forced to realize what it meant to be nearing the age of fifty, and the days of picking up and sweeping his wife off of her feet were over. He did not know when or how it had happened, but there he was, and it had happened, and he was suddenly old.

"George, I don't know how much longer I can do this. It has been hours. I can't, oh, God. Not another one." Melissa let her words trail off as she clutched at her belly and began to crouch over at the onset of another strong contraction. The pain was blinding.

George asked anxiously, "I know that you said that you didn't need a doctor, and maybe you're right and it is enough to call on Elizabeth. Still, it is not too late to call on a doctor. That Doctor, Doctor Day, everyone in the city over there says that he is a really good doctor." George did not know what else to do. He was a rancher, a miner, and he was seeing some success in politics, and as such he had spent all of his time and had put all of his efforts into keeping up with his work. Working on the farm and working with stone and heavy metals were good and honest professions. But other economic factors impacted the wider region that year, and work had been slower for George during that summer. Still, he was willing to call for a doctor if Melissa needed or wanted one.

"No. No. It's passing. The contraction is almost over. You have already called for Elizabeth. That will be enough." Melissa took several deep breaths before stretching her spine and standing upright. She took careful steps across what she called the main room, a simple living room with a simple red velvet couch, and a small, elegant-looking wooden side table that Melissa bought when she decided that she could not live without it while she was out on a shopping trip in Prescott shortly after they had arrived. There was a small window that faced the west and offered Melissa a wonderful view of the Bradshaw Mountains and Arizona's big sky. Melissa had paused to gaze out of that window several times over the year and had witnessed some of the most beautiful sunsets that she had ever seen.

George had paid a lot for the little cabin, and even though it did not have the white picket fence around it, and it did not have any trees around it at all, he had worked hard to turn the small three-room cabin into a modest yet comfortable house for his wife and their children.

Shortly after he acquired the homestead and the structure, he added several windows to the building in order to give Melissa a better and wider view to the outside. Melissa took one last look out of the window, focusing for a moment on the darkening mountains that were surrounded by expansive clouds colored with pink, crimson, and violet, and then she turned away and focused her energy on returning to her bedroom.

George was only a few steps behind her when she reached the side of the bed, and then he suggested, "you should probably get into bed. It won't be long until you start to have another contraction. You know how this works. It will only get harder and harder until the baby finally pops out."

Melissa tended to flail her hands about while she talked. The more dramatic her statement was, the more her hands would move. In this case, her hands flew out in front of her as she replied, "George, seriously. The baby does not just pop out. I have to push, for hours, until it finally squeezes out, and then there is more after that. Believe me, there is no popping the baby out of anything." As soon as she finished making the statement, she made a loud popping noise with her mouth.

George threw his head back in laughter. Melissa was laughing too. George agreed, "yeah, well, still. You do know what I mean to say though. The laboring part of this deal is only going to get harder.

"Yes, and I am getting into bed now because I know that it's time to lay down again." Melissa was cautious getting onto the bed so as not to disturb the coverings that George had placed carefully over the bedding in order to protect it. Melissa looked at a blanket and considered wrapping the soft fabric around her. Instead she decided to leave the blanket draped over the foot of the bed. The summer heat kept the cabin well above 80 degrees, and the thought of covering herself with a heavy blanket sent an uncomfortable hot shiver across Melissa's body.

"Liz, are you okay? You seem to be sweating a little more than you were earlier." George waited for a moment for Melissa to reply, but she remained silent and simply raised her right arm and used it to wipe off her forehead.

George stood up and moved to the corner of the room, where a white ceramic bowl that was filled with water was placed on a beautiful sculpted wooden vanity. He took a clean white washcloth from a pile on the top of the vanity and dipped it into the bowl of water, and then carefully wrung it back out. He took the cool, damp washcloth to Melissa's bedside, but when he raised the cloth in order to wipe and cool her face she recoiled and slithered sideways awkwardly across the bed, until she was in a position that was as far away from her husband as she could possibly get.

Melissa's face twisted as she squirmed and contorted her body away from her husband, and her voice boomed with frustration as she began to shout, "George, no! I don't want that thing on my face. No!"

George was confused and agitated by his wife's angry expression. George watched curiously as his wife writhed across the bed and then he asked confusedly, "Liz, what on earth are you doing? What is the matter with you?"

Melissa stopped wriggling and quickly sprawled out her arms and her legs so that she was flat on her back and laid perfectly still. She let out a loud sigh and looked up at the ceiling as she said flatly, "George, I have been watching the water and the environment around us change since we arrived. The summer season is the worst time of the year for the water, and I do not trust it. I know that you think that the water here is clean because all of it is moving through these creeks and streams throughout these rocky mountains."

Melissa took a deep breath, and then turned her head sideways to look directly at her husband and said, "George, it's not clean. The city that's over there, in Prescott, they are doing good. The hospital and a lot of the homes over there, they have water that travels into the buildings through pipes. They have wells and they have water, and they have sanitation, George. They have sinks, and they have bathtubs and showers, and they have toilets. Porcelain ones with pull chains that make the water flush and clean them out."

"I know, Melissa. I know. I have been there too, you know." George stood upright and took a deep breath and carefully observed his wife's face as he loosely clutched the washcloth in his hands.

Melissa looked back at George, glancing down at his hands for only the briefest moment before locking her eyes with his. She held his gaze as she shook her head gently from side to side, and then placed her hand over her bulging belly as she stated, "I'm tired of this, George. I don't want to have to go out to fetch our drinking water from barrels, and I don't want to go outside to use an outhouse anymore. I want to move out of here. I was reading the newspaper yesterday, and I saw an advertisement for a house that is for sale in the new Bashford addition. I was hoping that you might be willing to at least consider it, or perhaps you might at least consider a house that is similar to it. It's a big furnished house with an additional lot that is suitable for another structure. It has a functioning permanent well- which means that it has clean water. The best part is that the seller only wants 550 dollars for it all. It's actually a pretty good deal for what they have to offer."

George was taken aback by Melissa's suggestion and stammered in reply. "Liz, that's, I mean, you're talking about 550 Morgan dollars, and that is just a whole lot of money. I know that our family is growing, but"

Melissa cut George off in midsentence by stating, "that's right. That is exactly why we need a bigger house. A house with plumbing and sanitation, where I can keep the kids safe and healthy, George."

George let out a small gasp and then smiled awkwardly. "Melissa, yes, our family is getting bigger, and you're absolutely right about the fact that we need a bigger house that has all of that stuff that you want. But if we want a bigger house, then I need to be able to make more money. I think that we should talk about getting another mining cabin." As George spoke, he looked at Melissa with a concerned expression.

Melissa's eyes widened with shock, and her eyes narrowed down as she asked her husband through an annoyed tone, "George, do you honestly think that this is the best time to start talking about buying another mining shack?"

"Yes. As a matter of fact, I do." George replied with an air of confidence that Melissa had never heard from her husband before. His chin rose, his back straightened, and for a moment, he took a look forward and caught a glimpse of a future that only he could see. With a second cabin, preferably closer to the mines and closer to the smelters, George would be able to take on more work in more of the local rural areas where mining was still a thriving and growing industry. George wanted the chance to look for gold for himself. All of his time in Arizona had been spent on blacksmithing, raising livestock, transporting livestock for other ranchers, and moving metals for other miners. George was eager to create an opportunity that would allow him to search for some of the precious metals for himself.

He could see it clearly, a small shack somewhere along Lynx Creek where he would be able to work and look for gold. On the long summer days, his wife and his children could go with him, and they could sit outside, and as they cooked their dinner over an open fire and under the big sky with a billion stars overhead, he would tell them stories about their grandparents, and about the good old days and what life was like growing up in Canada. Every day would be a chance to find a little more gold. If he could just find some gold, he would have the money that he needed to buy Melissa one of those houses that she liked so much in the city. A house with a white picket fence and a fancy porcelain toilet.

George took a short breath, and in a reaffirming tone he said, "Liz, I know that it sounds crazy. But it makes sense to me, and it makes good business sense. I've done the math and I think that if we had another place to set ourselves up, somewhere not too far from one of the creeks, we would have access to a better water supply. If we are a little closer to the mines, I can shorten the distance that I have to ride every day. I will have a little more extra time, and that would allow me to make everything that I am doing a little more efficient and a little more profitable. Plus it would make it a lot more convenient to mine and look for gold because I can mine it and process it right there on the side of the hill, right next to a shack. We can grow our farm, grow our efforts to transport both livestock and minerals, and look for gold, and I promise you that I will buy you the house that you want in the city in almost no time at all."

George watched as his wife's expressions changed and soften as he spoke. "Why is it that you always come up with these wild and crazy gold mining ideas when I am trying to pop out a baby?" Melissa said with a small giggle and then closed her eyes as the most peaceful smile spread across her delicate face, just before the pangs of labor captured and stole her breath from her.

Melissa had only just begun to grunt and bear down in another contraction when they heard a sudden commotion taking place with the children coming from within the living room. As soon as Melissa was on the end side of the contraction, she shooed her husband away, asking him to check on the children.

George entered the living room to find that Elizabeth had arrived, and that the children had come out of their bedroom in order to allow her in. George watched as the children greeted their neighbor. He was amused by the children's clamoring voices and their effort to take the lightweight coat that Elizabeth was holding loosely in her hands.

Elizabeth surrendered the lightweight jacket and then questioned the children, "oh, I probably won't even need that old jacket, it's so warm in the summer. But I brought it just in case I need to stay and help into the early morning hours. So tell me, how is your mother doing?

Where is your father? Oh, I have to tell them about the news that I have heard."

Elizabeth heard the noise caused by George entering the living room, and without pause turned to face the shadowy bedroom doorway and asked warmly, "George, how are you? How is Melissa?"

George smiled and said, "I am doing well. Melissa is also doing well considering the circumstances. Everything seems to be coming right along without any problems."

Elizabeth flashed a wide smile that exposed a row of perfectly straight upper teeth as she replied, "that is fantastic. I am truly happy to hear that. I know that I need to be focused on Melissa right now, but I need to ask you if you've heard the important news this week. Just about everyone in town is talking about it since it was in the newspaper the other day. They are pushing really hard to reopen the mines. That McCrum character, he was in town this week and he said that all of his mines are ready to go because the level of the river is way up. He said that it was going well for his guys that are already out there back to work looking for that placer gold. They're expecting all of the mines to be open, and all of the miners should be back out there working by early next week."

George smiled shyly at Elizabeth's unorthodox nature and the way that she gave life to the story that he had already seen in the newspaper. She was not as eloquent as Melissa, nor as striking in beauty. Still, there was something special about the woman, and George had grown quite fond of her. She had proven to be a faithful friend, and a wonderful neighbor, though the Hassayampa camp where Elizabeth was living was somewhat of a distance away and it took her a half of an hour to ride the distance to reach George and Melissa's home.

After telling George of the news, Elizabeth took off her hat and allowed her short golden-brown hair to flow over her shoulders. She surrendered her hat to the children who were already eagerly waiting to take it from her, and then she asked about Melissa, "well, shall we get down to this other business with your wife and your baby then?"

George chuckled at the way that Elizabeth furled her nose as she smiled, and then he asked, "are you ready to come back into the other room to see Melissa? She has been waiting for you."

Elizabeth nodded in agreement and followed George into the bedroom where Melissa was already bearing down in hard labor. The children could vaguely hear their father talking as he closed the bedroom door behind him.

The children waited patiently as they listened to the noises that came from within their parents' bedroom. They played with their toys, occasionally looking up at one another, particularly when they heard a loud scream from their mother. The children noticed that their mother would scream, and then it would become silent. This cycle of screaming followed by silence went on for at least an hour.

Though they were young, they noticed the change when their mother had stopped screaming and everything had become quiet, and the silence lingered on. There was a heavy eeriness clinging to the silence that the children could feel lingering in the air as they waited to hear any sort of a noise from their mother. The longer that the quietness went on, the heavier the tension in the room became. The children were patient for some time, but having had enough of the dreary silence, they became restless quickly. Little George was the first to muster up enough courage to go to the bedroom door and to check on what was happening.

The young boy was cautious not to make any noise, and carefully placed his ear against the wooden panel. When he was not satisfied with the silence that he heard from within the room, the little boy carefully pushed on the door and cracked it open just enough to take a peek inside. And when the door swung open enough to give the little boy a clear view, he saw that Elizabeth was seated on a leather covered wingback chair beside his mother, who was lying on the bed, and he could see the profile of his father, who was standing at the foot of the bed and cradling a newborn baby boy.

Little George pushed the door wide open at the sight of his father, and the hinge of the door let out a high-pitched squeak. The squeal that erupted from the door was all that it took to get the other children excited, and they all simultaneously jumped up from their seats and sprinted through the door and into their parent's bedroom in order to capture the first precious glimpses of their new little brother.

George, the proud father asked as he looked down and smiled at his newborn son, "what are we going to name him?" George observed and admired the soft, smooth skin and the creamy color of his little boy's face, and the small patch of soft, fine brown hair that lay perfectly flat on the top of the baby's head. He turned his focus towards his other children as they lined up at the foot of the bed around him, and he smiled proudly as the children took their first look at their newest sibling.

Melissa smiled at her children, and then shifted her gaze towards her husband and asked, "I've been thinking about it for a while. Would it be okay with you if we named him after one of my brothers?"

"What do you mean? You only have a couple of brothers. Which one were you thinking about naming him after?" George smiled as he joked with Melissa. He could not help but feel some sense of concern over the suggestion. Melissa was one of fourteen children, and she had seven different brothers with twice as many names to choose from.

Melissa reached out to George so that he would hand the newborn baby over to her and stated, "let me see him."

As George slipped the newborn infant into Melissa's arms, Melissa looked down at the baby's tender face and said, "you know, from the moment that I saw his beautiful little face, he reminded me of my brother. I think we should call him Archie. What do you think of it, George?"

Melissa held her gaze on the newborn and did not wait for her husband to reply. Instead, she continued, "Archie. It means bold and brave, which is what we are all going to need to be when we get that second shack, cabin thingy."

George threw his head back and laughed. As he calmed himself, he smiled warmly at Melissa and looked down at his newborn son, and then turned and said excitedly to his older children, "welcome your little brother, Archie, to the world!"

Chapter 6
September 10th, 1899 - Walker, Arizona

By the time George was ready to leave the house in Walker, the roosters were already screaming and making a significant amount of noise. George looked around the room inside of the small house and thought about how much work they had all put into creating a stylish and comfortable home for Melissa. Though it was not located in the city of Prescott, the large windows and the spacious rooms were appealing enough at the time to get Melissa to agree to allow George to make the purchase just a year after their son Archie, was born.

George looked through a tall window on the east side of the room and caught a glimpse of the rising sun along the horizon, and shouted across the little house, "guys, come on, we need to go. The sun is rising, and the corn isn't going to pick itself. The eggs aren't going to collect themselves. The sheep aren't going to sheer themselves. The cows aren't going to drive themselves. Let's go, let's go, let's go, guys!"

Robert, William, Harry, little George, and Archie appeared from the darkened hallway one at a time, each one rubbing the sleep from their eyes as they joined their family in the living room. Pearl was the last to enter the main room, and she proudly announced, "my job today is going to be to help mama with the chickens and the eggs, and then later on today we are going to get some sweet corn from the market."

Melissa smiled and replied in a melodic tone, "that's right, my little Pearly girl. The train just brought in a full cart of that fresh and delicious, sweet corn yesterday, and I can't wait to go and get some of it."

Melissa paused and then said to her youngest sons, "Archie, Little Georgie, I want you both to go and get dressed so that you can help your sister outside with the chickens."

Both of the youngest boys shrugged and exclaimed, "no, come on mama, we don't want to take care of the chickens. We don't want to stay here. We want to go with Dad." Their little voices whined in synchronized unison.

Archie eventually turned and left the room to do as his mother had asked. Little George was more determined than his sibling was and decided to stay and question Melissa further about the decision. "Why can't I go and help Dad? All he is going to do is complain about the roads that he has to fix, and then he is going to dig some holes. And when he gets done with that, he is going to move some animals and get them ready to go to the train station, and when he gets tired of doing that, he is going to work over the fire while he beats up on some metal with a hammer. Just like he always does."

Melissa stifled a laugh and then she smiled and said gently, "sweetheart, I know that you think it's fun to go out there and work with your father, but it is going to be another sizzling hot summer day. I really don't want to have to worry about you out there in the summer heat." Melissa looked down at the young boy's face. Melissa thought that the boy shared a perfect likeness with his father. He had George's bright blue eyes, and he had his same dark, thick hair. Little George had all of the same smooth and soft, yet strong Scottish features that his father had, and he had none of his Mother's European characteristics, except for a few small, faint little freckles that ran across the bridge of his little button nose.

"But, Mama, I don't want to stay here and take care of the chickens. I couldn't go with Dad at all last week because of the rain from the stupid monsoon storms, and now you want me to stay here because it's going to be too hot outside. But I can't control the weather, and I just want to go and do some real work with Dad. Please, mama? Please, let me go with Dad." Little George begged of his mother and then looked towards his father for support.

"Liz, I can take him with me for the day. He can ride with me, and I will make sure that he stays safe. Everyone knows who he is, and someone is always keeping an eye on him. He has never given me any trouble, and in fact, he is old enough now that I can use his help, if he is up to it of course." George gave his son a quick wink and then turned his brilliant smile towards Melissa.

"I am! I am up to it!" The little boy proclaimed enthusiastically.

Melissa looked down at her little boy, who was beaming with pride. Melissa's hardened face began to soften as she took a long, deep breath, and gave in. "You already know what I think, and I don't like it. He is still far too young to be out there playing and working in that dangerous environment. He doesn't have a lot of life experience yet, and he might not recognize all of the dangers that are out there. But, if that is what you want to do," Melissa turned away from her husband to look at her son and then continued, "then I am going to trust that you will look after one another, and of course, you can go with your father. You should go and get yourself dressed and prepared for the day then."

"Yes! I'm going to go and get changed and into my work clothes!" The boy felt a small sense of victory and clenched his fist, flashed a toothy smile, sprinted across the room, and disappeared from view within a matter of seconds.

George watched Melissa's features closely, and he recognized her expressions as they changed. He watched her giggle gently at her little boy's gestures as he left the room, and then he watched her features harden, becoming very serious. He knew that she was concerned, and he also knew that she was displeased with the decision.

"I know that you worry about the kids, Liz. But you know that he is a very smart boy, and you can see how excited he gets. I saw Mr. Robinson after he and his wife got back into town the other day, and he was going on and on, talking about how great it is to see a young man with George's intelligence and ambitions. He said that his own children were older teenagers before they expressed any interest in learning how to help him out with anything on their farm, let alone mining and gold panning. To be honest, it sounded to me like their children's interest in it was mostly forced." George looked at his wife with raised eyebrows and a teasing smile as he finished the sentence.

Melissa turned away from George and looked out of the tall square east-facing window. The first glint of sunlight had begun pouring into the room, flooding the space with soft, warm, golden light. Melissa took a deep breath, tried to push down her fears, and smiled to herself as she explained, "I'm not concerned about his intelligence. He is as smart as they get. What I am concerned about is that this is a new claim and it's a new cabin, and even though we have all travelled through the area and we have been on all of those trails, we have not spent a lot of time in that particular area. We don't know very much about the new place. It doesn't help that the weather has been very unpredictable. I don't want any of you getting sick from this heat."

Melissa let out a deep sigh, shook her head gently and continued, "well, the public schools will be reopening on Monday, so it will only be a few more days before things will be back to learning and back to business. Once school is in session, then I won't have to worry about him out there in the desert heat as much." Melissa smiled peacefully. George knew that Melissa's children meant the world to her.

Melissa continued, "at least it isn't far from here. That kid, he just loves everything about that whole mining claim. I am glad that you finally caught up with all of the paperwork and got it registered with the county last month. Still, no matter how much he loves it out there, if the roads are still out, then you are going to need to take more time and extra precautions getting there. Please, you're going to need to be incredibly careful."

Melissa spun around quickly to face her husband and continued, "everyone in town has been talking about all of the monsoon storms that we just had. Everyone is saying that they haven't seen storms like this since the big storms of 1893. These recent storms created a tremendous amount of damage. It destroyed one of the reservoirs, and Mrs. Kennedy sent a message yesterday to report that the storm that rolled through this area just this last Sunday washed out most of what was left of the roads going into Prescott. She said that most of the roads are nearly impassable."

George let out a loud chuckle and then stated with a sly and cunning smile, "Liz, the roads might be bad, but they really cannot be considered impassable if Mrs. Kennedy made it through and into the city."

Melissa's hands dropped to her sides, and her voice became sultry and pouty. "Yes, she did make it. That is true. But, George, she said that the roads are rough, and I am just worried about the impact that it might have on you and the children. It is my job to make sure that you and the kids are safe. That's all."

George watched the expressions change on Melissa's face. He gave his wife a simple but proud smile and then stated, "it's my job too, Liz. I understand and I share in your concerns. Taking care of the kids and taking care of the roads, these are my jobs too. You have to remember that I was elected to oversee the roads in this district, and I take all of my responsibilities very seriously. I know that the weather washed everything out and the roads are still rough, but they are dry enough to get through. There will be teams of people out in the field working to fix the roads over the next week or so. It is a good thing that we had so much rain, because in all honesty, I have never seen the miners with more work than they have to do now. Between the gold that we will be moving into the city this week and the abundant supply of rainwater, the monsoon storms are turning out to be the best things that have happened in this desert in a while."

George paused and thought about how much his life had changed since they had arrived in Arizona. When they arrived in Prescott, they had only a few boxes in their possession. Over time, he was appointed as a deputy and elected as a Yavapai County Supervisor. He acquired five different gold-producing mines, and he laid claim to two homesteads. In less than a decade, George had successfully established himself as a miner, a blacksmith, a merchant, a lawman, and a politician.

George smirked, turned his focus towards his wife, and continued, "just think, with the roads all washed out and messed up, this is where we're fortunate that we don't have to worry about driving one of those fancy electric automobiles. The roads are bad enough that we wouldn't be able to use it. The horses can manage the roads, though it's probably going to take a little longer than it usually would to get to the cabin and to get into town. But if we had an automobile and no horses, we wouldn't be going anywhere." George smiled and raised his hands upwards with his palms turned upright, as if he were asking Melissa to agree with his point of view.

Melissa smiled playfully as she spoke, "you aren't wrong. If we had an automobile, it certainly would not be particularly useful to us right now. Still, I think I would prefer to have one as opposed to not having one."

George chuckled in amusement and turned to look out of the eastern-facing window. The sun was rising quickly along the eastern horizon, and it filled the room with warm, bright sunlight. They were silently watching the sunrise as the roosters screamed some seemingly very important messages in the background, and only a few more moments passed by when Melissa and George heard the children shuffling back into the room from behind them. Little George was the last to enter the space, and he proudly announced, "I think we are all ready to go, and we are just waiting for you, Dad."

Melissa laughed innocently at her little boy, who was usually more assertive than all of the other children. Melissa turned to watch her husband, who was also laughing, and then she said, "just be careful out there. Take your coffee, your canisters, and your stuff. And keep our babies safe. Bring them all back home to me." Melissa brushed her hand gently against George's arm, and George placed a delicate kiss on Melissa's left cheek.

George turned and walked towards the door, grabbed his hat from a hook beside the door, and as he walked out of the door he said reassuringly, "Liz, I'm going to do it."

Chapter 7
September 10th, 1899 - Lynx Creek, Arizona

George was seated on a short-legged wooden stool, and he looked across the small cabin and outside towards a thermometer gauge. The afternoon sun had quickly brought the temperatures up to the peak heat of the day, and the increase in humidity made the heat feel more extreme. George had already been working and sweating profusely within the four walls of the small cabin for several hours. It was to his dismay that the thermometer was showing that the temperature was 98 degrees Fahrenheit.

George stood up and stretched his sore and tired back. He was fatigued, and under the heat of the day, he needed something that would help to cool him down. He took a sip of water from his flask, and he knew from the weight of it that the small tin container was nearly empty. He looked around the room and decided that everything that he wanted to do would need to wait.

George stepped out of the doorway and took a deep breath. Though there was not much by way of trees near the cabin, there was a scenic panoramic view of the mountains that George appreciated. George took in the beauty of the natural, high desert landscape for a moment, and then he looked towards the west side of the cabin where his son was hard at work. Little George was using a shovel to dig a hole in an area that his father had often said might have a vein of quartz and placer gold running through it.

"Little Georgie, you sure are working hard over there. What do you say we take the Silver horse over into town to get some food and some more water? You never know, we might even run into your mother at the market. Come on, son." George looked at his son while he nudged and nodded his head towards the horse.

Little George dropped the shovel and sprinted across the yard towards his father. "Dad, guess what? I'm almost ready to pan a sample of this dirt that I was digging. I hope it shows some gold."

"Yeah. Me too buddy." George looked over towards the hole that his son had been exploring and gave it a quick half smile, and then continued to move across the yard and towards the hitching post. The horse was excited to see the little boy and let out a gentle whinny. Since the horse was still saddled up from the morning, it was already prepared to carry them the short distance into town. George mounted the horse first, and then he lifted his son from the ground and placed him on the saddle directly in front of him.

When the boy stopped adjusting himself and appeared to be settled, George asked him, "are you ready, son?"

"Yeah, Dad. I'm almost big enough to ride this horse all by myself. With the right stir-ups, I could probably do it." Little George looked down to see that he had grown and that his feet were getting near to the stir-ups. It reminded him of an advertisement that he had seen in one of his mother's newspapers, and the little boy remembered reading about the company and how they promised that the length of the stir-ups could be adjusted or changed to accommodate smaller childish sizes.

George rolled his head back and he let out a hearty laugh. Though he thought that it was funny, he also knew that it was true and eventually agreed with Little George, that the child would be riding the horse on his own very soon. George had already been through it a few times with his other boys who were already growing up, and they were off on their own horses, working as ranchers for the Orchard Farm, which was only about a mile away from their little Lynx Creek cabin.

George smiled and shook his head as he replied, "yes. Indeed you will, son."

George clutched at the reigns in his hands and squeezed his legs gently against the horse, and the horse jerked itself forward. The sound of the horse's hooves on the dirt road rang out loudly in little George's ears. The boy was delighted by the sight of the animals that scurried along the ground as they passed by, and the colorful red and blue birds that took flight as they made their way down the length of the trail and to the bottom of the foothills. The little boy noticed the blue jays, cardinals, ravens, and hawks circling in the air, and he spent a significant amount of time observing a prairie falcon. On the ground, he spotted two distinct species of rabbit, a packrat, and a squirrel. Even though it was not visible, he could smell the pungent odor of a skunk in the area nearby.

The recent rains caused the foliage to spring to life, and the small desert shrubs had grown and were more than six feet tall. Everything was thick, lush, and dark green, and most of the plants were blooming with bright yellow, orange, or red flowers. Others that bloomed showed deep blue or rich amethyst colors. Everywhere that the boy looked, the desert was putting on a brilliant and colorful show.

The little boy yelled out, "Dad, I smell a skunk, and it sure stinks. But the mountains and the foothills are beautiful out here. I can't believe how many flowers there are!"

George nodded and smirked as he said, "that's right, son. Even though it's the desert, you don't have to look very far to recognize that this is God's country."

The little boy fell into silence as he thought about what his father had said. He looked at the soft billowing clouds along the distant horizon, and then back down towards the brilliant and colorful plants that lined the pathway ahead. As he observed the mountains and the perfect earth around him, he began to understand what his father meant.

It was only a mile ride, and when they arrived at the market, George helped his son to make the dismount from the horse before he swung his leg over and eased himself off of the horse. George made sure that the horse was securely tied to the hitching post in front of the market storefront before turning his attention back towards his son. Most of the hitching posts were open, though there were a few other horses there, including a white horse, a spotted brown horse, and an unusually tall horse with lanky brown legs and a long pale face. Little George looked up at the giant pale-faced horse, and then down at his 8-year-old legs, and he wondered how old he might be when he would finally be tall enough to be able to ride a horse of that size.

George noticed that his son was evaluating the horse and also himself, and then he said encouragingly, "I see you looking at that big draft horse. Don't be discouraged. You'll be able to ride a horse like that someday. Right now you might not be tall enough to ride him, but someday, someday soon you will be. Until then, you are just going to have to stick close by me and Silver." George gave his son a reassuring smile and waved his hand to gesture for his son to follow along.

George and his son entered the little market, where the little boy marveled over the halved barrels that were filled with seasonal produce, and the shelves that housed a variety of jars filled with eggs, pickles, jellies, jams, and spreads. When they found the barrel that was filled with the farm-fresh sweet corn, George said to his son, "your mother said that she was going to come here today to try to find some sweet corn. Maybe we should pick some up for her? And we need some for us."

The little boy's eyes widened with excitement, and he vigorously shook his head in agreement at the suggestion, and he said, "yeah. That sounds good, Dad. Mom will like that." The little boy had the most content smile as he spoke of his mother.

Melissa always said that little George looked just like his father. However, though the little boy strongly resembled his father, he also shared a distinct likeness with his mother. As George looked down at his little son, he could see the shape of Melissa's eyes and the sharpness of Melissa's chin. His speech patterns, the cadence in his tone, and the way that he enunciated certain parts of a word or a statement, as far as George was concerned, the little boy was just like his mother.

George and his son stood in front of the half barrel that was filled with the seasonal, fresh sweet corn. The husks were still tightly wrapped around the cobs, and Little George was fascinated by the shiny yellow corn silk hair that was protruding from the top end of the vegetables. The little boy extended his stubby little fingers out in front of him to touch the corn silk, and he was surprised to find that it was stickier than he thought it would be. He had expected it to feel like his mother's hair- smooth, silky, and strong. The little boy decided that it felt nothing like his mother's hair. Though it did feel silky, it was mostly wet and sticky, and he was surprised to find that the fine yellow strands were surprisingly fragile and were easily broken.

George watched his son in amusement and then turned his focus towards picking out the freshest cobs of corn. "Son, you pick out four, and I will pick out four. That should be enough corn for everybody to last a day or two. Make sure that you pick out the ones that have the brightest green and have the tightest husks, and make sure that there aren't any little brown holes in any of the husks."

It only took a few moments for them to select the corn. When they each held four cobs, they turned and looked around and began to notice many of the different items that were for sale that they had not noticed before. Little George had seen the milk, the butter, and the beef, but he was curious about the cans that had a variety of different and colorful labels that he had never seen before.

As they casually walked through the small market and approached the cash register, Little George read the labels on the colorful cans, "Dad, there are canned dried beans, canned dried nuts, canned barley, canned alfalfa, canned cereal, and they even have canned coffee. You like coffee." The boy pointed his tiny index finger at his father, squinted, and gave him a wide smile that displayed a mouth full of beautiful baby teeth, with the only exception being the two front larger adult teeth.

"Good afternoon, Sir. Young man." An older woman greeted the pair from behind the cash register. George placed the corn down on a small table in front of the woman, and it occurred to George that he had never seen the woman before.

"Will this be everything for you gentlemen today?" She looked up at George as she spoke and suddenly realized that he was quite a handsome man. Though she was not necessarily interested in him, he was attractive enough that she took the time to tend to her looks. She adjusted her scarf and primped her gray-blonde hair to make sure that it was still coiled up neatly and resting on the top of her head.

"Yeah. I mean, no, Ma'am. I also need to get some water while we are here. I need to fill my canteens and my jugs. Is the stream running enough to get the well to pump?" George tilted his head and looked up at the woman's face in anticipation of the answer. George was truly hoping that the woman would say that the well had been repaired and was working.

The woman smiled quaintly and then replied, "we have had a lot of storms. The monsoons have been terrible. The stream is up, but we have been having problems with the well and with the pump for a while now, so I am really not sure about how fast it will pump. However, now that the water level is higher than I have ever seen it, it should work well enough to get some water out of it. You are welcome to go back there and to give it a try."

George slipped some money into the woman's hand and paid for the purchase. George gave the woman a warm smile, and then he nodded and tapped the rim of his hat with his index finger and replied, "great. Thank you kindly, ma'am."

George gingerly scooped up the ears of corn from the table and turned to walk out of the market with his son following closely behind. Silver was excited to see them exit the market and make their approach, and the horse let out a soft, breathy whinny. George moved steadfastly to the side of the horse and opened the leather saddlebag. The saddlebags on the horse were responsible for transporting the jugs and the canteens of water, a bedroll, and a few other items that George felt were necessary and were light enough to carry.

George carefully placed the corn into one of the big leather bags and took out the water containers, and then told his son, "If you want to, you can stay here with Silver while I go out back to see if I can get these canisters filled up."

"Can I sit on the saddle?" Little George's eyes were squinted nearly shut as he looked up towards his father, who was standing with the sun behind him.

"Yeah, but you know the rules about sitting on the horse. You have to keep it tied to the post, and you cannot give it any signals that might startle it. You don't want it to try to take off running while it's tied up, especially while you're on it." George looked down at his little boy, who was growing up entirely too quickly.

"I can handle it, Dad." The little boy said firmly with his chin tilted upward. He was a confident child, and it made him all the more endearing.

"Okay, let's get you on up there." George chuckled and put his hand out to help aid and boost his son onto the saddle.

"No, Dad. I can do it by myself. Watch." The boy then proceeded to grab the side of the saddle, hoisted his leg high up into the air until his foot caught the stir-up, and then with all of his might he pulled himself up until he could reach the horn of the saddle with his right hand. With a hand on the horn, the boy pulled himself up and over the saddle, and had himself seated and positioned properly with relative ease considering his small stature.

George was taken aback by the effort that his son had put into getting onto the saddle. "Well, Excellent job. You did that better than those kids do over at that cowboy camp." George laughed and tickled his son's side as he teased him. The cowboy camp was a place for the city people to go that came for a visit and wanted to know what it was like to live and work out in the country, and to sleep outside under the stars. The people that visited the cowboy camp were often easy to identify, and the cattlemen who were true cowboys often made jokes about the city slickers that showed up to take part in the coordinated events at the camp.

"Okay, I need to get serious and get these things filled up. I'll be right back behind there." George stated as he pointed in the direction of the market, implying that he would be behind the structure.

"Okay, Dad. I'll be right here." Little George pointed downward to the horse on which he was sitting. The boy watched as his father carried the containers and then disappeared behind the wooden building.

Chapter 8

September 10th, 1899 - Lynx Creek, Arizona

George placed four filled water containers into the leather saddlebags, closed the covers, and cinched them closed. George was perspiring, and the warm breeze that filtered through his clothing did little to cool him down. He took a small drink of water from the flask that he carried in one of his trouser pockets.

George noticed that his son was also perspiring under the heat of the sun, and he handed the flask to the boy. "Here, son. Take a drink and then hold onto that for me while I get up there on the saddle with you."

George untied the horse, and then he took great caution when mounting the horse, gently stepping around his son until he could lower himself onto the saddle behind the boy. George had plenty of practice riding with the children but mounting the horse while one of the kids was already seated on the saddle required a little more caution and a lot more attention.

The little boy tilted his head back and took a long drink of the cool water. When he was satisfied, he placed the cap back onto the flask, waited for his father to position himself in the saddle, and then held the flask out to return it to his father. George took the canister from the boy and slipped it back into an oversized trouser pocket and then asked, "are you ready, son?"

"Yeah. I am ready. Let's go, Silver!" The little boy cheered as George gently squeezed his legs against the horse, and the horse slowly turned and began to trot back down Main Street.

With the additional weight of the water, the horse moved slower, and the ride back to the cabin was slow going. The sun was scalding, and the ground was holding and radiating heat. Little George felt overwhelmed by the heat, and so he failed to notice the cottontail rabbits that scurried by as the horse turned down the path to head north. He did not notice the roadrunner chasing a lizard, nor the quails that scurried across the road in front of their horse. Instead, the quiet gallop of the horse's hooves drummed on like a tender lullaby that had been written just for the little boy.

George noticed that his son was swaying in the saddle in front of him, and he hollered, "are you falling asleep? We are almost there, son. We just need to make it another two minutes north, and then we'll make the small curve, and we will be at the cabin." The horse made a right turn to head north on the trail and up the foot of the hill, and towards the small cabin.

The little boy snapped back quickly to an awakened state and replied, "yes. No. I don't know. It's too hot out here, and I'm just a little bit tired." The boy focused his attention on a covey of quail as they scurried from underneath a thick bush as the horse moved by. He watched, and he wondered what it would be like if he had wings and he could fly as freely as the birds overhead, hovering above the trees, and sailing for miles on a gentle whisper of a wind. The boy abandoned the idea when the horse trotted up to the front of the cabin and stopped abruptly at the hitching post along the short fence.

"Okay, son. I'm going to climb down first, and then I'm going to let you get yourself down." George stood upright in the stir-ups and swung his leg over the back of the horse and dropped down to the ground, one leg at a time. He waited close by and watched as his son practiced the same footsteps that he had used. Because his son's legs were just a little short for the dismount, the little boy nearly stumbled off of the saddle before he found his footing on the ground where he steadied himself.

With his son's dismount complete, George grabbed the reins and tied the horse to the hitching post. George then shifted his focus to unbuckling the saddlebags, looked down at the corn, and then at the containers of water. "We need to be careful with this water. It's still pretty hot out here, and we still have a couple of hours before your brothers will be back after working at the orchard farm. Remember that it's okay if you need some water but try not to use more than you need.

And don't use the clean water for testing your gold pans over there." George said as he nodded towards the area where his son had been digging earlier in the day.

"I was thinking that I would use one of the extra horse troughs for that, Dad. They all still have a lot of water in them from the rain and the monsoon storms. Sometimes Silver and the other horses drink from there, so I can try to be careful, and I won't get any dirt into the trough." Though he hadn't asked it as a question, the little boy looked inquisitively at his father as he waited for a response.

"Yeah, use the one that is the farthest on the left. It's only about twenty feet or so from where that hole is that you have been working on, and there should be enough water in that extra trough for that." George nodded his head yes in approval and gave his son a little smile. He was proud of his son. He was proud of all of his children, naturally. But there was something about little George and his temperament and his demeanor that made the child adorable, and it made George feel proud. The child was incredibly charming, and George had a special bond with his little boy because of it.

"Do you want me to help you to take the water in first?" The little boy asked as he pointed towards the canisters in the saddlebags.

"No, I can get it from here. But, before you run off, I want you to take this with you in case you need it." George reached into his trouser pocket and took out the flask that he had already filled with clean drinking water.

"Here you go." George said as he handed the small metal container over to his son. The little boy eagerly took the flask and then George turned his back on his son while reminding him to, "be careful over there."

George grabbed as many water containers as he could carry, and then made the short walk up the pathway to the cabin door where he placed the containers in the shade underneath the front awning of the small wooden structure. He stopped for a moment in the dreaded heat and wiped his sweaty face against his sleeve. After a few moments, George walked back to the horse to retrieve the last of the containers and glanced over towards his son on the west side of the house. The little boy was already using a shovel to spear and chop at the earth and had already moved another cubic foot of dirt from the hole.

"Good job, son. At this rate, you'll be halfway to China by tomorrow." George shouted to his son teasingly as he continued to walk the short distance back to his horse.

The little boy stood upright sharply and then turned towards his father and stated firmly, "it doesn't work like that dad. It's not even possible to dig my way to China."

George let out a roar of a laugh, and then told his son, "I know, son. It was just a joke. I just meant that you're making really good progress with that hole."

George smiled and then turned his full attention to the task of ensuring that the horse had access to the water troughs. When he was certain that the reigns were tied up at the correct length, he turned to retrieve the last of the containers that were holding the water that they needed. After removing the last of the containers from the leather bag, the saddlebag flopped itself closed. George took a deep breath and felt invigorated by the musty leather smell, and then turned to walk back towards the cabin. As he stepped under the small awning, he wiped his feet, smiled proudly, and then entered the small doorway into the cabin.

George looked around at the space inside of the small cabin and decided to leave the door wide open. While they were in town, the cabin was closed and sealed up underneath the summer sun. The temperature inside of the cabin had increased rapidly and it was almost unbearable. It was absolutely sweltering.

George placed the containers onto the wooden floor in one of the darkest corners of the room. He wiped the sweat away from his forehead using the back of his arm and then leaned against a small worktable that he frequently used when he needed to weld metal. It wasn't luxurious, but, between the worktable, the dining table, and the cabinet, the space inside of the shack was suitable enough for what they needed it to do.

George stood there for a moment and tried to remain inside of the cabin before deciding that the heat inside of the room was simply too intense. He turned and stepped out of the front door and walked the short distance around the cabin on the east side, and he didn't stop until he reached the south side of the cabin where he had his forge and all of his larger tables and anvils.

George looked down at his forge, and then over towards his largest anvil. He was dreading the work that he knew he still needed to finish. He was tired of the heat. He was tired of the rocks, the dirt, and the dust. He was tired of the fire, the forge, and the smells and the noises that came from both hammering and welding metals.

George took a deep breath and clumsily sat down on a pine log bench that he made for himself shortly after Melissa had agreed to allow him to buy the cabin. With his back to the cabin, he gazed over the view along the southern skyline and focused on the sun that was shining brightly over the hills, and he noted that there were only a very few sparse white clouds that were stretched and spread thinly along the distant horizon.

George muttered grimly to himself, "so this is what it's like getting old. You set off with a dream, and if you work hard, really hard, maybe something might work out for you. Or you will just wind up tired, to the point that you might wind up being tired of being tired. And then one day you wake up and realize that you're tired because you're old." George leaned back against the bench to rest his sore and tired back. He was frustrated.

George took another long, deep breath, and then thought of his wife and his children. Though he was frustrated, he looked across the quiet, serene valley, and he could not help but to feel thankful to be able to work for himself. It was true that he was tired, but at least he felt like he had the power and the control that allowed him to do something about it.

Just as fast as George had started to feel bad for himself, he sat forward and was back up on his feet and stated with clarity to nobody in particular, "time to get this work done so that we can get back home to Melissa on time today."

Chapter 9
September 10th, 1899 - Lynx Creek, Arizona

Little George was deep in thought. He had been listening to his family talk about gold mining for almost all of his life. His father had talked about things like getting down to the bedrock or finding black sand, or a vein of quartz, and how they needed to follow those veins in order to find the gold. According to what everyone in town said, there was supposed to be a lot of placer gold in the area where they had their cabin, and the boy knew that if he just kept digging, eventually he would find it.

The sun was bearing down hard on the boy, and he perspired heavily as he worked under the passing sun. After a while, he had no choice but to stop and to find some shade to rest in. The little boy crouched down in a cool, shady spot behind a row of short native shrubs and opened the water flask that his father had given to him earlier in the day. He pulled heavy from the flask at first, and then he remembered how his father had said that they could not waste any of the scarce and precious resource. He cut off his sip, gulped down the mouthful of water, and found that the small amount of water was just satisfying enough to quench his thirst. His small hands worked to twist the cap back onto the flask, and then he carefully placed it back into his lower front denim trouser pocket.

The boy rocked backward in his crouched position until he fell slowly backwards and landed on the ground in a seated position. He giggled to himself as a thin cloud of powdery brown dust wafted out from underneath him. He turned his attention back towards the hole that he had been digging and then decided that he was nearly ready to test some of the dirt samples. The boy justified it by considering that the heat was relentless, and if he tested the samples, the coolness of the water would make the work more bearable and more tolerable. But, if he tried to go back to digging the hole, he would be working in the sun, and it would require him to drink a lot more of the clean drinking water.

The boy stared at the hole and decided that he would rest for just another moment. He was enjoying the short break in the coolness of the shade. The little boy was amused by the lines and the shadows that were made by the sun and the wild shrubs, and he kicked his legs straight out in front of him across the dirt and the rocks. The sun pelted his legs, and it quickly warmed up the boy's denim pants.

The boy stared at the denim material, and it reminded him of a pair of denim trousers that his mother had once bought for him. He remembered how he had put them on when the temperatures were high, and he thought that he would be able to cool himself off by creating small air vents that would allow the air to flow in and out of his trousers. He remembered how it felt to hold the sharp stone in his hand, and how tedious it had been to drag the stone over the knee of the blue fabric until the fabric was weakened enough to eventually give way to a hole. The little boy smiled as he remembered how proud he had felt when the hole had finally appeared, and then again when he was strong enough to widen the hole with his very own bare hands.

The boy's smile turned into a deep frown as he recalled how angry his mother had become when she saw the torn knees in his jeans. He remembered how her face had scrunched up and turned red with frustration, and how her voice cracked as she shrieked frantically, "what did you do? I just bought those denim trousers last week! So help me. How am I supposed to keep all of these kids safe when I can't even keep them in proper clothes!"

The little boy looked down at his knees and gazed over his thin legs hidden behind the fabric of his trousers. The boy waved his feet from side to side and observed his small shoes peaking out from the ends of his pant legs, and even though he was miserable in the heat, he made the decision to leave the knees of his trousers intact so as not to upset his mother.

Having had enough of the break, the boy slowly climbed up and raised himself into a standing position. He clumsily brushed off the dust from his trousers and walked over to the hole that he had been digging.

The boy walked around the hole and over to an area next to a patch of small thorny desert shrubs where there were a few things that he had been collecting and playing with over the long summer, including some gold mining pans, a small bucket, a small hoe, a short-handled rake, and a full-sized shovel that his father had given to him just before the monsoon season had arrived. He picked up one of his small mining pans from the ground and shook it off and watched as a small tuft of dust fell from the pan and blew away in a gust of wind. When he was satisfied that the pan was suitable enough to be used to test his dirt, he placed it on the ground beside a small wooden bucket. Then the little boy picked up the bucket by the handle and flipped it upside down, and he was quite amused by the warm sludge that oozed out of it.

The boy moved over to one of his dirt piles and leaned down over it, and then used the gold pan to scoop up a small amount of the dirt. The boy carefully poured his hand-selected dirt into the bucket. He looked down at the contents in the bucket and then added a little more dirt. As soon as he was satisfied with the amount of dirt that he had to wash and process, he grabbed the bucket by the handle, and while still clutching the pan, he made his way over to the extra water trough.

Little George placed the bucket beside the trough, looked down into the water below, and wondered how many things he might be able to think of that were made up of the same color as the dirty, rusty, cloudy water below. Frustrated by the appearance of the dirty water inside of the trough, the little boy shook his head gently from side to side.

The little boy took a step backward, looked at the water and then his dirt piles, and he reconsidered the exact process that he wanted to use to wash the selected dirt. He thought about running the dirt through the water in the trough, but he had already promised his father that he would keep the dirt out of the trough. The little boy eventually decided that his initial inclination and his father were correct, and the trough already had enough problems on its own without him adding any dirt to it.

After a moment, the little boy picked up the bucket and dumped the contents into a pile on the ground beside him. Then he placed the bucket into the trough, filled it with water, and then pulled it out from the trough and placed it on the ground at his feet. Using his gold mining pan, he scooped up a small amount of dirt from the ground and dunked the pan with the dirt into the bucket of water. The young boy pulled the pan back up quickly, allowing some of the dirt and gravel in the pan to spill out into the bucket. Then he sloshed the water and the dirt in the pan forward and away from him, and then back and towards him. He tilted the pan from side to side, and he repeated this process several times until there was only a small amount of dirt and a small amount of water remaining in the pan.

The little boy lifted the pan from the bucket and tilted it slightly so that the dirt and sandy material spread thinly across the top of the pan and then fountained downward slowly across the surface of the pan. He pulled the pan closer to his face, tapped it several times, and carefully inspected the liquid and dirt material to see if there was any showing of gold. The little boy squinted his eyes tightly and peered closely at the pan, and he fought back a wave of disappointment when he did not find any trace of gold in the pan.

Though he was disappointed, he was determined to find the gold that everyone he had ever known said was in that ground. He was determined to find it, so he tried the process again. The boy filled the pan with dirt and then dunked it into the bucket, flooding the pan with water. Then, the boy moved his whole body to shake the pan from front to back, and then from side to side. His small hands tapped against the sides of the pan, just like his father had taught him. As he washed the dirt from the pan, the boy hoped that he would begin to see a few small flecks of fine gold. Yet again, the pan only showed a cascade of fine dirt and silt.

The little boy was undeterred. He tried again, and again. Eventually, his small dirt pile dwindled to nothing, and he realized that he was going to need to shovel and dig more dirt if he was going to continue. With that decision, the boy flipped the bucket onto its side and drained the dirty, muddy water from it, and then he took the bucket over to the hole that he had been working on and clumsily dropped the bucket beside it. The boy picked up his shovel, and the heat from the wooden handle immediately burned and irritated his small fingers. Still, unwilling to be defeated, he carefully re-gripped his fingers around the handle of the shovel and scooped up a fresh amount of dirt. The boy hastily shoveled the dirt into the bucket.

When he was finally satisfied with the amount of dirt that he had collected, he dropped the shovel onto the hard ground beside him and reached for the bucket handle. As he lifted the bucket, the boy thought that the contents of the bucket felt much heavier than they had before. It was more challenging for him to carry, and he lost his balance and stumbled when he attempted to lift it. He might have fallen to the ground if he had not been agile and lucky enough to regain his balance and catch himself from falling. He did not know how long it had been since he had started washing the dirt, but he knew that it had been some hours and he had become quite tired from working under the heat of the afternoon desert sun.

As he approached his makeshift panning and washing station, little George abruptly let go of the handle and allowed the heavy bucket to drop to the ground at his feet nearby the trough, where it landed upright with a thud. The little boy took a small, awkward step backward and away from the bucket, and stopped in his place while he attempted to catch his breath. The boy reached into his pocket and retrieved the small tin alloy flask that his father had given to him earlier that afternoon. He carefully unscrewed the top and then placed the small container to his pursed lips, tilted his head back, and closed his eyes while he savored a sip of tepid water. The boy felt the last of the water empty from the canister just before he pulled it away from his mouth. The boy looked at the empty container in his hands for several moments before replacing the top, and then stowed it away in his trouser pocket.

The little boy turned to look towards the cabin and considered going inside where he might be able to rest and cool down. Instead, he wiped his face onto the back of his sleeve and turned back to face the bucket of dirt and the water trough. The heat was daunting, and the little boy could not keep the beads of perspiration from forming and rolling into his eyes, which blurred his vision. He wiped his face again, and then grabbed the bucket firmly by the handle.

Little George became confused when he realized that he barely had enough strength to lift the bucket. He tilted his head sideways and looked disappointedly down into the bucket of dirt before letting out a deep sigh. As he stared down into the bucket, he began to grow frustrated, and then decided that there had to be another way, an easier way, to gather and to move the dirt that he wanted to process.

The boy looked around the yard and glanced at all of the old tools that he had inherited from his father over the summer. He thought about his options for several moments before turning his attention toward the empty flask that he was still carrying in his pocket. Because the flask was empty, the little boy thought that it might be useful as a tool in his dirt washing operation. The little boy thought that if he could fill the flask with water, it could be poured over the pan and the dirt, and it would be a more efficient use of his water supply.

He felt a sudden rush of energy, and he sprang to life as he hurried to reach for the pan that was placed on the ground beside him. He used the pan to scoop up a small amount of dirt from the bucket, and then he placed the pan on the ground immediately in front of his feet. When he was satisfied with the position of the pan, he cautiously unscrewed the flask and dunked the metal container in the trough. The boy smiled as tiny bubbles appeared from the small container, and floated upwards, breaking at the surface of the water. When the bubbles stopped and the container was filled, he carefully pulled the flask out of the trough and then poured half of the contents from the flask over the pan. Then, he picked up the pan and moved it around, rocking it back and forth, cautiously adding a small amount of water at a time until the flask was empty, the dirt was cleared, and the pan was showing thin, fine streaks of cascading dirt and silt.

Chapter 10
September 10th, 1899 - Lynx Creek, Arizona

George was not exactly certain of the time, but he knew from the position of the sun that it was somewhere around 4:00 in the afternoon. The fire that he had stoked up in his forge earlier in the afternoon had already cooled down, though it was still smoldering and radiating an amount of heat. He considered using the last of the heat from the fire to boil some rainwater that he had collected in a large wooden barrel during the recent monsoon storms. However, he dismissed the idea and decided that it could wait since he was able to get water from the well in town earlier that day.

George looked eastward out over the rolling foothills and paused as he focused on the new Humboldt smelter standing tall to the south-east side of town. Every time that he looked at it, he was reminded that everything that existed in the small town had all been built because of the mining, and that everyone living in the area was connected through the mining in some way. Life as a miner had proven to be difficult, given that the previously constructed smelters had been closed and had only reopened earlier in the year after long and arduous legal battles over the damage that the mining had caused to the groundwater, the environment, and to the health and the lives of the laborers.

This new smelter stood for the promise of a return to mining, and it was expected to bring in new opportunities and more work for more people. George had noticed that it did bring in more people. However, he also noticed that it had not created many new jobs for the people that had already been living there. George scoffed at the thought, turned away from the smelter, and focused his attention back on his workspace.

George paced the ground behind the southside of the cabin and looked around at his workspace. He ensured that his tools were properly organized and ready for the next morning and then focused on ensuring that the fire was down and that everything would be safe to leave for the night. George wanted to leave the cabin as soon as the older boys returned from their workday and given the lateness of the hour, he knew that they would be along shortly, and it would soon be time to return home to Melissa.

George looked over towards the west side of the property where little George was crouched down with a mining pan in his hands. George thought that the young boy had been unusually quiet throughout the day. Yet, every time that he had gone to check on the boy, he found the child to be hard at work with his bucket and his mining pan, and he made the conscious decision to allow the boy to have the freedom to play, to explore, and to discover and learn about the natural world around him.

George had a soothing, deep voice that echoed gently across the foothills. "Georgie, son, how about you come on into the cabin, and we can get you wiped up and ready for the ride back home. As soon as your brothers get back, we are going to jump on the horse and head home so that we can arrive before the sun has fully set. We also need to get that sweet corn that we bought for your mother home before it dries out too much and it starts popping."

"It won't do that, Dad." The little boy replied in an agitated, stern tone.

George laughed heartily as he replied, "I know that it won't do that, son. I only meant that I don't want the corn to go bad because it was left in the saddlebag for too long. You know what corn does when it is left in any kind of a container, especially when it is warm, wet, and in the husk?"

The little boy perked up, turned his head to look at his father, and yelled out the answer, "it will start to grow mold!"

"That's right." George smiled proudly as he assured his son of the answer. "If the corn is left in the bag for too long, it will start to sweat, but really what the corn goes through is condensation. And it is the heat combined with the condensation that creates the humid conditions and the perfect environment for the mold spores to grow."

George continued talking to his son as he walked around to the front and the north side of the cabin and became slightly distracted when he noticed that a siding board near the doorframe of the cabin had come loose. George let out a long and heavy sigh as he looked closer to inspect the problem and discovered that a nail head was bulging outward and was protruding from the aging wood.

The little boy noticed that his father had become distracted, and he pushed himself up from the ground and brushed off what dirt and dust that he could from his clothes. Then the boy turned the water flask upside down to empty it out onto the ground beside him and placed the cap tightly back onto it before slipping it back into his pocket. He placed the mining pan into the dirty and mostly empty bucket, and then took his work items and placed them beside the hole where he had been working. He hurriedly dropped the bucket and the other items and turned to run towards the cabin.

The boy slowed down as he approached the cabin, and hung his head low as he announced sadly, "Dad, I hate to tell you this, but I didn't find any gold." The boy frowned heavily as he spoke, and he slowed his approach, stepped onto the porch, and stood quietly beside his father.

George let out a loud, sturdy laugh, and told his son, "I hate to tell you this, son, but finding gold usually takes more than one or two days. I didn't expect for you to find any gold."

"What? You didn't expect me to find any gold? How can you even say that? You said that there was placer gold in that area, and I didn't find any of it. Not even one little speck." The little boy squinted his eyes and held out his hand with his fingers in the shape of a zero. It was clear from his tone that the little boy was frustrated.

The child continued to complain, "nothing. Zilch. It's completely kaput."

George continued to laugh at his little boy and then said warmly, "I'm sorry. I know that it isn't funny, and I don't want you to feel discouraged, son. Believe me, I know exactly how frustrating it is to put in all that time and effort into looking for gold only to find a pan full of nothing. But eventually you are going to figure it out. If you keep looking, I promise you, eventually you will find gold."

George opened the door to the small cabin and stepped inside. Little George followed his father into the cabin and closed the door behind him while he continued to complain, "but I have been looking. I worked hard to look for it today, and I didn't find anything. If I want to have anything in life, like some big horses, or a house or anything like that, then I am going to have to be able to find gold."

George moved around the room as he began to tidy it up. He smiled and nodded his head as he said, "well, that is how gold mining works, son. Some days the gold is in the pan. On most days, it's not. But there is one thing that every miner eventually comes to understand along the way, and you might not understand it just yet. But you should know that most of the miners that wound up being successful, most of them generally didn't come here empty-handed. Sure, there are the determined and lucky few. You'll read about them in the papers. But most of these guys that got lucky, they had a different day job and at least a little bit of money to get started. To be really honest with you, son, most of them had a lot of help."

George looked squarely at his little boy as he finished the sentence and then reached for one of the water containers. George took the water container and moved across the small room towards the lonely, small cabinet that was fixed to the southern wall. The cabinet held a few small cups, a few oddly shaped plates, a few forks, and a few knives. George pulled out two of the small cups and filled them to the brim with fresh water.

"You were working hard out there, son. I saw you working, and I want you to know that I'm proud of you for putting in that kind of effort and for not giving up on it too soon. Mining and panning are both challenging. And if you want it to pay off, then you have to keep going and you have to keep looking." George stopped and took a sip of water from his glass and then placed the other glass onto the table in front of his son.

George continued, "and I know, son, there really is nothing worse than putting in all that time and energy into the effort of looking for gold and not finding it. There is nothing worse. I know it."

George decided not to discourage his little son any further with the full context of the truth, that he had felt the same disappointment himself more times than he could count. He had bought the larger cabin in Walker, but it didn't have the water service or the sanitation that Melissa wanted for the children, and it was merely intended to be a steppingstone towards more opportunities since it was a suitable place to live while they established themselves by working and looking for gold. When the cabin at Lynx Creek became available, Melissa was reluctant to register the homestead claim. Still, she didn't really ask for much of anything, and she had never denied George of anything that he wanted, which was to look for gold. George had looked for gold, and he was always surprised when he was lucky enough to find it, because more often than not, he did not.

George took a deep breath and continued, "sometimes, all you can do is start again tomorrow. It's hard, but you have to stay motivated until the next day, and then you have to be just as excited when tomorrow arrives simply because you have another opportunity to look for gold. If nothing else, when you're all grown up, you won't be stuck ranching or working for some farmer, since you already have the skills that you need to go to work for a mining company. Maybe you can even start a mining company of your very own."

George had been looking for gold for a long time, and he believed that gold fever was a unique characteristic, and that you either had it or you didn't. He had it, and it was absolutely clear to him that his little son also had it.

The little boy took a hold of his glass and took a quick sip of the water and said, "there's nothing wrong with being a cattleman, Dad. I like the cows and the sheep, and I can work around the animals just fine. But I really want to find some gold because then we will have enough money to buy more cows and more sheep. I don't really know if one job is better than the other. I just know that I want to keep looking for gold."

The little boy paused for a moment, and let out a short sigh before asking, "do you think that mom will let me come back out here with you again tomorrow?"

"Of course, she will, son. As long as there are no monsoon storms, she'll give in. She says the same thing every day, but I think that she will likely allow you to come out here with me for the next few days since you will be back in school next week. You should know by now that she is the way that she is simply because she loves you and because she worries about you."

George sat down in a chair next to his son and leaned in towards the boy and gave him a gentle, loving smile, and continued, "it is what your mother does."

Little George smiled and tilted his head shyly. Then his head tilted to the other side and his smile flattened into a thin line. The little boy let out a gruff noise and then said, "Mom is too worried sometimes though."

George laughed gently at his little boy, and then said, "yeah. Probably. But she has good reason to worry about us. This is coyote country, and you can't forget that this area was named after the lynx lion for a reason. Your mother is right to be worried about things like rattlesnakes, scorpions, black widows, and the countless other things that are skulking around out here that might kill you if you should happen to come across it. And I can tell you for absolutely certain that your mother is going to be worried about us if we don't make it back home before dark tonight. So, what do you say we refill our packs and get ready for the ride home? Do you still have my flask?" George had been carrying and using the flask as a water canteen since before his little boy was born. It had served him well over the years, particularly during the long, sweltering summer days.

"Yeah." Little George said as he enthusiastically hopped up from his seat and reached into his pocket. He pulled the flask out and held it out for his father to take. "Here you go." The boy felt a strong sense of pride because he had been able to hold onto the flask, and he smiled proudly as he handed the flask over to his father, and then sat back down in the chair.

As George took the flask from his son, he heard what sounded like horses approaching from the dirt road and suggested, "that sounds like your brothers are coming back in. Let's get our stuff together and get ready so that we can head back home as soon as they get here. This way they won't even need to get off of their horses."

The little boy picked up his glass of water and finished it. He put the glass down on the table, stood up, and gathered a few trivial things from the table, paying particular attention to a small, wooden toy horse that had been given to him by a young girl earlier in the summer. The little girl's name was Hannah, and little George was pleased when he learned that she was exactly his same age. He had really taken a liking to the young golden-haired girl, and as he held the toy in his hand, he silently hoped that he would get to see the little girl at the public school that was scheduled to begin the next week, and then he quietly slipped the toy into his pocket as he turned to look at his father.

George stood up and considered what he was going to need to take with him on the ride back. He shook the flask and was surprised to find that its contents were completely emptied. George unscrewed the flask, and carefully filled it with fresh water from one of the larger containers. The flask did not hold a lot, but the small amount of water was useful during the summer months. When it was filled, George placed the cap back onto the container and tightened it firmly.

George held the flask out for his son to take, and said, "I am going to give this back to you for safekeeping." The little boy reached back out towards his father and took the flask into his tiny hands. The boy smiled proudly as he slipped the flask back into his pocket.

George focused on putting the water containers back into their storage area, then picked up the two empty glass cups from the table and quickly wiped them off with a rag, and then returned the glasses to the small cabinet. When he was satisfied with the tidying, George looked around at the space within the cabin. It had been an organized mess when they had arrived that morning, and because it had been so hot during that day, nothing much had changed and it was still the same organized mess.

George recognized the sounds that he heard coming from outside of the cabin, and he knew that his oldest sons were returning home. "Son, why don't you go and meet your brothers out there at the hitching post and tell them that I want to get going right away and that they shouldn't even bother getting off of their horses." George nodded at his son and looked towards the front of the cabin and at the doorway.

The little boy was quick to respond to his father, and he broke out in a run as soon as his feet were outside of the doorway. He sprinted the short distance from the front door and out to the hitching post. Though he had given it an effort, his brothers had already made their dismounts, and the three horses were already tied up on the post beside the Silver horse by the time the boy crossed the short distance to reach his older brothers.

Disappointed by his failed effort to intercept their arrival, the boy turned to make his way back towards the cabin. It had been a long, hard day of work under the relentless sun, and the sun had again been waiting to brutally assault the boy on his short run to the fence line. He moved slowly, and he stopped on the porch to take cover under the small awning attached to the front of the cabin. He could hear the clamor of his brothers talking, catching little bits of information about their day. He was frustrated, tired, and sweaty, and he decided that he was not interested in any of his older brother's current concerns. The boy was too busy feeling disappointed after the last of the day's blazing heat left him exhausted. He was tired, and he was parched.

Chapter 11

September 13th, 1899 - Lynx Creek, Arizona

George reached across his worktable and picked up the watch that he had dropped there earlier in the morning. It read three minutes after two. George dropped the watch back onto the table and wiped his forehead with the back of his other arm. He took a couple of long, deep breaths and looked towards the work that he had already completed, and then towards the forge. Beside it was a pile of metal pieces and other raw materials that he planned to use for his work that he still needed to begin.

It was a warm morning, and the temperatures throughout the valley climbed rapidly as the day moved into the afternoon hours. The heat was making George feel weak and tired, and he was certain that little George was ready for a break. The little boy had run off to go and search for gold as soon as they had arrived that morning, and he had been out working in the heat for most of the day.

George thought about the morning and how his older sons had stood around the hitching post for a couple of extra minutes before they took their leave for work, and they had innocently laughed about the little boy having more ambition and more energy than they all had combined.

George stood up from his stool and stretched his arms and his back. He turned to walk the short distance around to the west side of the property and continued to explore the ground and the surroundings until he reached the area nearby where his son had spent the week digging and looking for placer gold. George found the little boy sitting on the ground, holding the pan in his hands which were resting on his lap.

George looked down at the boy and suggested, "why don't you come on inside of the cabin and get something cool to drink, son. It's really hot out here, and we should probably try to cool off for a little while until after the sun passes over."

"Okay, Dad." The boy replied as he lazily dropped the pan and watched it fall onto the sun-bleached dirt beside him, and then he clumsily got himself up and onto his feet.

George gestured for the boy to walk with him towards the cabin and said, "let's get you inside and get you cooled off."

The little boy walked over to his father, and after they took a few steps towards the cabin George said, "try not to be too discouraged by the showings in your pan today, kid. If you keep at it, eventually you're going to find a whole lot of gold in your pan."

The little boy looked down at the ground as he walked with his father. He had not told his mother or his father that he was not feeling well, nor that his stomach had been bothering him since the prior evening. He was afraid that if they knew that he was having stomach problems and was feeling generally unwell, then they might have decided that he was not in good enough condition to go with his father to the cabin for the day. Still, throughout the day his stomach slowly became swollen with pain, and he did not want to admit to his father that he had not worked any of the dirt that morning because of the pain that he was experiencing.

The boy took a deep breath and said, "it's not that, Dad. It's just, I don't know. I just feel kind of clunky today."

They stopped briefly under the small awning of the cabin before entering the small space to find that the cabin was only slightly cooler than it was in the outdoor environment. George took off his Stetson hat and tossed it gracefully onto the small worktable, where it landed flatly. He snickered at the hat and then turned to face his son and said, "it's stuffy in here, but even the one- or two-degrees difference should make it a little easier to cool back down."

The little boy sat down on one of the two chairs, wrapped his left arm across his abdomen, and took a deep breath. The pain in his stomach had become worse, and it had become tender to the touch. The boy clutched his hand against his abdomen, hoping that it might somehow work to ease his pain, and instead he found that every action only seemed to make his pain and discomfort worse.

George focused on retrieving two glass cups from the cabinet and let out a small chuckle as he spoke to his son, "your mother, she used to say that she hated the cold in the winter. Let me tell you, when we went through the first winter here and it snowed, your mother nearly lost her mind. Fortunately, there wasn't much snow that year, and we learned from that first season that it generally melts off by the next day. They get more snow in Prescott than we do down here at this lower elevation. Not to mention that the winters are far milder here than they were when we were living in Canada. When we were living in Canada, she would go on and on for months about how miserable she was in the cold. She would complain about how it was so cold that it would make her hair freeze and break right off. And it was true. I saw it happen. Twice."

George reached for a large container of fresh water and filled the two cups that he had pulled out of the cabinet with the fresh drinking water. He smiled and shook his head as he spoke, "it has been a while since she has had to go through one of those cold winters. But now she says that she prefers the dark, cold winters over the extreme heat that we have here in Arizona during the summer. Working out there in that heat today, I almost hate to admit it, but I might be forced to agree with her."

He put the large water container down, took a small step towards his son, and slid one of the cups that were filled with water onto the table in front of the little boy. George placed the other cup to his lips, tilted the cup back, and took a long sip of the cool refreshing water and then continued, "your mother likes the fair-weather days. If it's anything below 70, she will say that it's too cold, and if it's anything above 70, she'll say that it's too hot."

The little boy tried to focus on his father's words, but the pain in his abdomen overtook him. His father continued to talk as the perspiration began to bead up and fill the thin lines that ran across the little boy's forehead. The boy clutched at his stomach and attempted to alleviate the pain, but he was in so much pain that he could no longer be exactly certain of what it was that his father was talking about.

George looked down at his little boy under the light of the dimly lit cabin. It took a moment for his eyes to adjust, and he was surprised when he noticed that his son had developed a small, pink-colored spot on his right cheek. The spot was about two centimeters in diameter and formed an almost perfect circle.

George tilted his head as he looked down curiously at his son and then asked, "are you okay, son? You haven't touched your water, and you've had even less to say than you've had to drink. What's going on with you?"

The little boy sat silently and did not acknowledge his father's questions. He was consumed with the pain that he was feeling, and he was no longer certain of what he was supposed to be doing. He was confused about what his father had been talking about, he couldn't be certain about where he was, and he didn't know what he was supposed to be doing. Suddenly, nothing made any sense to the little boy.

George was immediately concerned by his son's silence, and he quickly grabbed a chair and placed it beside his son and sat down. He looked at the boy closely and then asked, "what's going on? Are you overheating? Or did you get bit by a snake, or a spider, or something? There's a spot or a thing on your cheek."

The little boy shook his head rapidly and tried to focus on coming out of the haze that had him trapped. He focused on his father's voice, but it took time for the recognition to set in. "No. I don't know. Nothing happened. I don't know. I'm just really tired, and I don't feel well." The little boy's eyes drooped heavily as he spoke.

"Okay. Well, that's okay, son. Do you want me to get you a bedroll, and then you can lie down and get a little rest?" George asked his son softly, placing his hand on the back of the boy's neck to pat him and to attempt to reassure him that it was acceptable to rest during the day if he needed it. George was shocked by what he felt. The boy's temperature was so high that it caused George to recoil.

George looked at his son, and his eyes pulled into a tight squint with concern. After a brief moment, he said, "I think that you have a bit of a fever, because it feels like you are burning up. So I am going to need you to drink some of this water for me, and then I am going to need you to get those clothes off. I'll go and get you a bedroll, and then you can lie down with a damp, cool cloth on your head. If you are overheated, you'll feel better soon. It could also be that you have caught one of those seasonal influenzas. Regardless, it's pretty much the same protocol. You need to get some of that water into you, and then get your shirt and your trousers off, son. You get yourself undressed, and I'll go get the bedroll. I'll be right back."

George stood up abruptly and took a few steps towards the doorway, opened the door to the little cabin, and left the boy alone in the room.

The little boy watched as his father walked out of the door, and then he looked skeptically towards the cup that was filled with water and was placed on the table. The thought of drinking the water sent pangs shooting through his stomach. His father had also told him that he should start undressing. He could do that, he thought to himself.

The boy clumsily unbuttoned his shirt, and before he could slip the material down and away from his arms, he became increasingly weak and no longer had the energy to carry out the simple task. He simply sat there, unable to muster up enough energy to finish removing his shirt, he conceded defeat to the task and allowed his arms to dangle loosely beside him. The boy closed his eyes and let out a dry cough. His breathing had become shallow, and he struggled to catch his breath.

Only a few moments passed by when his father reentered the cabin with the bedroll that he kept stored in the saddlebag on the horse. He kept it there so that he would always have a place to sleep in case there was ever an emergency or a need for it. He glanced down at the northwest corner of the floor, bent over to place the bedroll on the ground, knelt to unfasten the tie, and then unrolled the makeshift bed. When he was satisfied with the bed, he turned his attention to his son while asking, "what do you think of that? It'll work for now at least."

George looked at his little boy and was as equally confused as he was concerned by what he was observing. George stood upright and took a few steps towards his son and looked down at the child, who was sitting silently with his shirt open. The boy had always been slender, but George felt a surge of panic while he was looking at the child's small frame and specifically at his bloated abdomen.

George looked closer and noticed that the boy had developed several of the pink-colored spots on his neck and his back. The spots were scattered in patches, and they were identical to the spot that George noticed on the boy's face after they came into the cabin. George was not certain about what might be causing the unusual pink or rose-colored spots, but he thought that they were similar to a rash that he previously observed on the older children when they had experienced a high fever.

"Dad, I don't feel good. Can I just go lie down?" The little boy looked up at his father from behind heavy eyelids, and glossy, pleading eyes. George noticed that the white surrounding his son's turquoise blue eyes had become completely reddened.

"Of course, son. Come on. I'll help you get into the bed and get you comfortable." George said as he held his hand out for his son, and the little boy took it. George noticed how small and delicate his son's hand felt as it was tucked inside of his own much larger hand. George looked at his son's little hand and thought back to the day that the little boy was born. George could see the baby's tiny fingers wrapping around just one of his own. He admired the delicate fingernails, and the tiny nail beds. George had thought at the time that it was the most perfect little set of fingers on the most perfect little boy that he had ever seen.

George helped his little boy to get up from his chair, and then to lie down on the makeshift bed on the ground. The boy curled up onto his side and did not say very much as he wrapped his arms around his stomach and tried to find a position that would allow him to feel a little bit of relief. Still crouching beside the boy, George said, "I'm going to let you rest for a while. If you need anything, I'll be sitting over there, or I'll be right outside. If you need something, just say something, and I'll come right back in. Okay?"

The little boy closed his eyes, took a deep breath, and exhaled slowly. George shook his head with worry when the little boy mumbled back, and his speech was nearly unintelligible. George thought that perhaps his son said something along the lines of, "okay, Dad. I am just going to sleep here for a while."

George stood up and looked down at his little boy. It was clear that the child was ill. What was not clear was what George could possibly do about it. George considered calling on one of the other ranchers or miners in the area for some guidance. George actually wanted to call on a doctor, but that would have meant leaving the boy alone for some time in his given condition since there were several cabins that were in the nearby area, but none of them were occupied by any doctors.

George eventually determined that the best option would be to wait for the older boys to finish their workday on the orchard farm, and then at least one of them could ride up to the Walker house and let Melissa know that little George was sick. Melissa needed to know that they were going to need to wait for a day or two for the boy to recover from the illness before they would be able to make the return ride back home.

George looked down at his son, who had already fallen asleep. The gentle sound of the boys breathing put George at ease. He watched the boy sleep for a while as he pondered how intelligent and clever the child was. The boy had proven himself to be intelligent, and a fast learner from an incredibly early age. He performed well at the public school, and he was at the top of his class, and ahead of all of his peers. Not only was he intelligent, but he was also incredibly charming. There was a natural easiness about the boy, and his charismatic nature made him both sociable and very likable. As George looked down over his ill son, he was reminded of how lucky he was to have such impressive, good-natured children.

After some time passed, George became restless and frustrated, and he no longer found any purpose in sitting around. Conceding to the reality of his son's illness, George decided that the only thing that he could do was to leave the boy to rest. He looked at his little boy and watched him for a moment longer, and then he went outside and to the rear of the cabin, where he would be able to focus on his forge and his work.

Chapter 12
September 13th, 1899 - Lynx Creek, Arizona

George attempted to focus on his work, but he was not able to stop thinking about his son, who was ill and resting inside of the cabin. He did manage to get some small tasks accomplished, but he was not able to function at an efficient level of production. He had stopped more times than usual to go to check on the little boy, and he was finding it to be incredibly difficult to concentrate on what he needed to do. He made several mistakes that caused the metal that he was working with to warp and to crack. He was frustrated with himself because of the mistakes, which felt like bigger mistakes than they actually were, and he was making these mistakes because he was highly distracted with worry.

Between the heat and waiting for the older boys to come back after work, the afternoon hours seemed to take an eternity to pass by. George felt a wave of relief when he finally heard the sound of the horses coming up the road and he knew that his sons were close to returning. As soon as he heard the horses, he shifted his focus toward cleaning up his workspace and shutting down his forge for the evening.

When all of his tools were organized and put away and George was satisfied with his workspace, he walked around to the front of the cabin where he waited for the older boys. There was just enough time for George to kick the dust off of his work boots when the boys walked up the short pathway to the cabin. They were carrying on loudly, joking and laughing about an unfortunate incident that had occurred earlier that day with another rancher, who had somehow managed to lose his trousers to a tiller.

"Boys," George stated abruptly and with a tone that was so sharp that it startled the young men and brought them all to immediate attention. They looked puzzled, but they listened intently to their father as he began to explain, "your little brother is inside laying down. I have been keeping an eye on him, but I am afraid that he's very sick. At first, I thought that the heat might have gotten to him and that he was either exhausted or dealing with the beginning of a heat stroke, but I have since realized that it is likely one of those seasonal influenzas that have been going around. It seems to go around every year during this time of year, and I recently heard a few of the people that work in town complaining about it. I honestly don't know what to think of it. He has been sleeping for hours." George looked down towards the ground, his eyebrows raised into high arches as he contemplated what might be wrong with his son.

George did not have all of the words that he needed to accurately explain the condition that his little son was currently in. He continued staring at the ground and then silently turned and began walking towards the cabin. His three older sons took his cue and followed him to the cabin and in through the narrow doorway.

George swung his arm wide and pointed at the little boy lying on the bed in the corner and shrugged his shoulders as he stated, "he's just laying over there, sleeping. He hasn't stirred in a while, and it doesn't seem like any of the noise that I make is bothering him. Our boots just made it sound like an army was marching in here, and that wasn't enough to wake him. You can see for yourself that he is very sick."

Robert leaned against a wall, Harry leaned against a chair, and William leaned against the edge of the table. They looked at their father and then at each other with confused expressions. Each of the boys took his time to analyze and process what they were seeing when they looked over at their little brother.

Robert eventually spoke and agreed with his father, "yeah. I mean, look at him. He's sweaty and he's very pale, and it's pretty clear just by looking at him that he's sick."

Robert stared at his little brother and thought about the situation for a moment, and then continued, "someone needs to go and let mom know that Georgie is sick. What if I ride back to the house with William?" Robert looked at William, who was already looking back at

Robert and was nodding his head in agreement with his older brother's suggestion.

George thought about Robert's suggestion for a moment and replied, "I had thought of that. I thought that I might send one of you up there to the Walker place to let your mom know that he's sick and that we just aren't going to be able to make the ride back home tonight. I was thinking of sending you, Robert, being that you are the oldest. But I don't want any of you out there riding alone. And, William, your horse is the strongest and the fastest. I think it makes sense if the two of you go so that you can ride together. It will make it a little safer at least. It's going to take about an hour for you guys to get back home to your mother, and I don't want either of you out riding after dark."

George spoke, and then watched as William turned to look at his little brother who was still sleeping on the bedroll.

William looked deeply concerned, and then he let out a deep sigh and said softly, "if we go now, we can make it there before dark. But because of the time, that means that we need to leave right now. And I do mean right now."

George felt the weight of his responsibilities as a father fall heavily onto his shoulders, and he exhaled sharply. He turned to look at his little son laying on the bedroll placed in the corner on the floor. He shook his head in disbelief and let only a few seconds pass by before he walked across the small room and quietly knelt down on the floor beside his son. He placed a hand gently onto the little boy's forehead, which caused the boy to twitch.

George said, "he's still burning up." Then he spoke directly to his little boy, "I know that you aren't feeling well, son. But I need you to wake up for a minute. You have an extremely high fever, and we need to get some water into you."

The little boy rolled from his side and onto his back. His shirt fell open and exposed his swollen, bloated belly. The little boy could barely open his eyes, and as he spoke, his speech became heavily slurred,

"Dad, my stomach hurts. I should have told you and mom sooner. I feel terrible. I should have told you that I was sick, and I should have stayed at home with mom."

George was taken aback by the rapid change and the rapid decline that he noticed in his son, and he was suddenly overcome with an escalating sensation of panic. His heart rate increased, his pupils dilated, and he immediately broke out into a cold, clammy sweat. He tried taking several deep, steady breaths, and he did everything that he could to stay calm and composed as he frantically asked his son, "what are you talking about? What do you mean, son?"

George felt a sudden rush of adrenaline. With it came a deep sense of fear as he watched his little boy mumble indistinctly and then drift back off to sleep.

"Boys," George's eyes were wild as he took a moment to think about what he wanted to say, and then he chose his words carefully. "Go get your mother. Just tell her that your brother is sick and that I need her to come here to the cabin because I need some help getting his fever down. That's it. Don't tell her anything more than that. She needs to know that it is important, but we don't need her to get herself into a rush and hurt herself on the way here."

William was the first to question the decision. "Dad, do you think that's the best idea? I mean, he is seriously sick. Sure, it's easy to tell us that we should tell mom that he's sick, but it's going to be a couple of hours before she will get here. The sun is setting, and it is going to become dark quickly, and that could be dangerous for Mom. Instead, don't you think that maybe we should just call on a doctor or take him to the hospital?" Seeing the condition that his little brother was in caused an alarm inside of him to go off, and William's tone had become increasingly edgy as he spoke.

George was irritated by William's tense tone, and he snapped back sharply, "I thought of calling on a doctor, but I don't know of one within a five-mile radius. Do you know of one within a five-mile radius?"

George paused for a moment and then let out a heavy sigh as he collected his thoughts. George calmed himself and then continued, "it is not going to be easy to get your little brother to a hospital. The train schedule is already done for today, and it would take too long to get there with the train anyway since there's no direct line from here into Prescott. Meanwhile, we already know that the roads were washed out and they are still rough after the monsoon storms last weekend, and it is going to be an awfully hard ride into the city in order to get him to the hospital. It will be one of the more difficult rides that we have attempted. So, the first thing that we need to do is to go and get your mother."

George looked sternly at his sons and said, "the two of you are going to ride together, and then at least one of you boys will need to be prepared to stay at the house with the younger kids. Tell your mother not to bother bringing a carriage because the roads are all still out. She can make it on horseback, but she will never make it if she tries to come down that trail with any sort of a cart."

George stood up, slowly, stretching his legs and massaging his knees along the way up. As soon as he straightened his back, he looked down on his ill son, and something about the condition of the boy caused George to quickly rethink his decision.

George shook his head from side to side and then he told his sons, "actually, William is right. We are not going to sit around here waiting for something to happen. The three of you, I want you three to go and get your mother, and as soon as you guys are gone, I am going to load your brother up with me on the Silver horse and I am going to start heading towards the hospital. I don't think it can wait any longer. I need to get his fever down as soon as possible. I have already waited to see if he was going to improve, and during that time he has only continued to decline, and he is declining quickly. I think that it's time to get some help, and so there is no sense in us sitting here and wasting any more time. This is my final decision. The three of you go and tell your mother that she should meet us on the trail, where the trail meets the road at the crossing near the camp."

George shook his head in disbelief, barely processing how quickly his son's health was deteriorating. He tried to shake it off and focused his thoughts on his little boy, and on how he intended to make his new plan work realistically.

George took a deep breath, and then looked sternly at his sons, and said calmly, "I'll get Georgie loaded up with me on Silver. I am going to run as straight on through as I can until I hit the downtown area in the city and I make it to that Gurley Street, where I'm going to turn and then I will follow the road north-west towards the hospital. Hopefully, your mother can meet up with me on the trail. If I don't see her on the trail when I make it to the crossroads near the camp, I'll drop a set of blacksmithing tongs on the trail at the crossing. I seriously doubt that I'll get ahead of you, but make sure to check the crossing. If you see the tongs, don't wait there. You ride on up into Prescott. And remember that when you get into the city, only the gaslights will be lighting the path. It is going to be very dark the whole way through the mountains, so do not miss the turns and do not get lost on any of these trails. Most importantly, stick together until you get all the way into Prescott and to the Sisters of Mercy hospital. Do not lose your trail!"

William was genuinely concerned about his brother, but also about his father. After all, he had noticed over time how his father's salt and pepper hair had become almost completely snow white. His father was no longer a young man. Planning to ride two-up with little George while the boy was in a fairly unresponsive condition only complicated the matter. William could not help but to be concerned. "Dad, are you sure that you want all three of us to go home? Don't you want someone to stay behind and ride with you?"

"No!" George clenched his jaw tightly as he replied sternly. "No. I want you three to leave together, and I want you three to stay together. It is going to get dark fast, and I need to know that nothing else is going to go wrong while I deal with this situation with your brother. My decision is final. You all understand what you need to do, yeah?"

George had to make a conscious effort to calm himself as he spoke to his sons. The children were helpful, but George wanted them to hurry while being safe, and in the wild desert and forest mountain landscapes, they would be safer if they traveled together. George decided that the care of his little boy was his responsibility. He would take care of the boy, and he would see to it alone that his son arrived safely at the hospital.

The three boys took only the briefest moment to say goodbye to their little brother. They told him to, "feel better soon" and to, "be safe on the journey into the city to see the doctor." The boys put on their strongest and bravest faces as they said goodbye to their father, and they took leave of the cabin.

George sat down on a chair and listened to his sons as they made their departure. When the last faint sounds of the horses hooves beating on the ground finally tapered off, George took a deep breath and then sprang into action.

He glanced down at his son's swollen belly and shook his head in horror as he leaned down and retrieved his flask from the pocket of the trousers that his son was still wearing. With the flask in his hand, George stood up and looked around the room, and then walked over to a small box that contained some clothing. He found a long-sleeved button-up shirt and pulled it out from the neat pile and then shoved the flask and the shirt sloppily into one of his pockets, allowing most of the fabric to dangle out.

George took a deep breath and looked around the room one last time. He felt overwhelmed, but he knew that he needed to stay focused. He went over to little George, knelt on one knee, placed his arms underneath the boy, and lifted him gently off of the ground. George pulled the boy up into his arms and held the boy closely against his chest. The little boy whimpered as George stood upright.

"Shush now, It's going to be okay, son." George whispered gently into his son's ear.

"Dad, I don't feel good." The little boy's voice sounded weak and broken.

"I know that you don't feel well, son. I'm going to take you to the hospital, where you're going to see a doctor, and he is going to have you feeling right as rain in no time at all." George spoke softly as he carried his son out of the cabin. Though his back was sore, and his knees throbbed, it did not matter. Nothing could have ever hurt him more than seeing his son become so ill that it would require an emergency trip to the hospital.

He carried his son out of the cabin, leaving his black Stetson hat on the table and allowing the door behind him to close itself shut. He walked cautiously towards the horse, and told his son, "Okay. I am going to put you up on Silver. I know that you don't feel well, but I am going to need you to help me out a little bit, Okay? When I get you up and onto the saddle, grab onto the horn, and don't let go. Do you think you can do that?"

George did not wait for the boy to answer. He hoisted the boy up and over the saddle, and the little boy's legs flopped onto and then over the horse until he was seated awkwardly on the saddle.

George grabbed his son's little hands and placed them on the horn and said, "you're supposed to grab this, son." George looked at his little boy and realized that because of the severity of the illness, the boy had already begun to drift off to sleep.

George anxiously bit his lower lip and shook his head from side to side, and then quickly untied the reins from the hitching post and mounted the horse behind his son as swiftly as he could. He reached down to find the shirt that he had stuffed into his pocket. He turned the shirt backward, draped the back of the shirt around the front of his son, and then put his arms into the sleeves of the shirt and pulled it up over his shoulders as far as it would go, creating a makeshift pouch that might help to hold his little boy in place while they navigated the difficult and washed-out roads. The last thing that he wanted to have happen was for his son to fall off of the horse where there were no resources, and while they were already on their way to the hospital to get emergency medical help.

George made sure that his little boy was secure in front of him, and then looked back over his shoulder at the cabin one last time before he squeezed his legs against the horse. He took a deep breath and said a short prayer for a safe journey as the horse began to trot. The journey was slow at first, but as soon as George was comfortable and certain that his son was safe and wouldn't fall off of the horse, he used his legs to give the horse a fast, hard squeeze, while yelling, "Yah! Yah! Go! Go! Go!" and the horse broke out into a fast gallop.

Chapter 13

September 13th, 1899 - Walker, Arizona

Robert arrived at the house first, though his two younger brothers, William, and Harry, were not far behind him. Robert was anxious after riding back to the house, and he was eager to find his mother and to tell her about what was going on with his little brother.

"Mom!" Robert was yelling and calling out for his mother before his horse had come to a complete stop. He was in such a hurry to find his mother that he forgot to tie his horse up. He jumped off of the horse and dropped the reigns, and then ran into the small house in a heightened frenzy.

Melissa was in the kitchen cooking over an open fire when she heard the horses coming in for the evening. She had thought that she heard one of the boys yelling, but they were always hooting and hollering and carrying on about something. She was not concerned about the noise until she heard Robert shouting and calling out to her directly from the front yard. She was wiping her hands against a soft cloth when Robert burst through the front door and startled her so severely that she nearly fell to the floor.

Robert was bold, and as he spoke, his tone was so sharp that it sent a wave of fear into Melissa's core. "Mom, whatever it is that you're doing, you need to stop, and you need to come to help Dad."

"Why? What happened to your father?" Melissa was wide-eyed, and even though she did not know what had occurred, she was already in a state of panic.

Robert took a few small steps towards his mother and said, "no, Dad is fine. It's Georgie. Georgie is sick and Dad is taking him to the hospital."

"What? The hospital? What are you talking about? What happened? In what way is Georgie sick? What's the matter with him?" Melissa's eyes were fraught with fear. As she questioned her oldest son, she scanned his face in an effort to see if he would give away any clue about her little boy's condition.

"Georgie is sick with a fever. Dad couldn't get the fever down, and it got worse throughout the day. The fever is concerningly high. Georgie is just sick, and I think that we all kind of agree that he needs to go to see a doctor right away." Robert stated, and then he took a moment to allow his mother to collect herself. Melissa listened to the explanation and quickly realized that the little boy must have been extremely sick, otherwise, there would have been no need for an emergency trip to the hospital. Melissa took several deep breaths and did her best to maintain her composure.

When he was sure that his mother was ready to hear it, Robert continued, "Dad wants you to meet up with him at the crossroads out by the camp. Dad and Georgie were supposed to be leaving the Lynx cabin just a few minutes after we did. They are riding two-up, so that will already set them back a little while. Based on my best estimate, they should be riding near the camp, and they should reach the crossroads for the trail and the road in a little more than a half an hour from now, depending."

Melissa looked down at herself and examined the apron that she was wearing to cover her neat and freshly pressed dress and shrugged as she said, "okay. Well, I am going to get changed, and then I guess I need to leave. It's probably going to be just after dark by the time I meet up with them on the trail."

Melissa turned quickly to leave the room and heard Robert shout from behind her as she made her exit, "I'll be going with you."

Only a moment had gone by when William and Harry entered the house. William's eyes were swollen, and his face was pale.

"William," Robert said as he quickly assessed his younger brother's overall emotional state, and then asked, "would you mind staying here with the other kids? They're in the bedroom. But someone needs to stay here with them while I go with mom to make sure that she is going to be safe. Because it's just," Robert let his voice trail off.

William felt the full weight of the circumstances of his little brother's illness fall upon him. His shoulders began to hunch, and his head hung low as he nodded in agreement and tried to blink back the tears as he said, "yeah. The trails and the roads are really bad. They are the worst that I have ever seen them going into town. I can stay here with the kids. But you need to make sure that Mom gets into the city safely." William looked at Robert and met his eyes. He was scared, and he was serious.

William shifted his stare over to his other brother and asked, "Harry, are you going to go into the city, or are you going to stay here with me and the younger kids?"

Harry shook his head for a moment and then said, "no, yes. I don't know. I am not sure what I should do. I want to go with Robert, and I want to make sure that Georgie is okay. But I also think that I might be of more use if I stay here to help with the younger kids. At this point, I don't know what I should do."

William took a few steps towards Robert and folded his arms across his chest as he said to his older brother in a whispered voice, "I don't know what to make of all of this. Dad said something about thinking that Georgie has some kind of influenza. I don't want to say that it isn't some sort of seasonal influenza, but I don't think that those were exactly the symptoms of influenza. I mean, did you see his belly?"

Harry listened to the quiet conversation intently before suggesting emphatically, "I think that William is right. I've seen lots of people get the flu lots of times. That didn't look like the flu to me either."

Robert snickered at the comment and then replied snidely, "you might have seen a lot of people who were sick and infected with influenza, or you might have even seen a large number of people who have had an influenza many times, but you've never seen lots of people get the flu lots of times, Harry."

Harry raised his hands in the air, his eyes widened, and he stated plainly, "you know what I mean. There are people that I know who have gotten the flu, and over the years the number of people starts to add up. They were all sick with some sort of influenza, and they sure didn't ever look like that."

Robert smirked but could not find it in him to continue the banter because he was not certain about what was wrong with his brother, and he did not want to encourage any further speculation about it. Robert replied softly, "all I know is that I heard in town the other day that the influenza is going around, and so it could be some sort of influenza."

"Who has influenza?" Melissa questioned loudly as she reentered the room and then stopped to wait for a response.

The boys looked at one another and searched for an answer that they might be able to provide for their mother. Eventually, Robert explained, "Dad said that Georgie might have some type of seasonal influenza."

Melissa's face twisted with confusion as she stated, "he didn't eat his dinner last night. And this morning he seemed to be a little quieter than he usually is, but otherwise he appeared normal. I suppose that some influenzas can set on fast, especially if it's one of those European or Spanish strains of influenza." Melissa did not know what to make of it. She only knew what she had been told, and what she had been told was that Georgie was sick.

Melissa continued, "okay, perhaps it is just a strain of influenza, but if the illness or his symptoms are so bad that he needs to see a doctor, then that is all the reason that I need to hurry up and go."

Melissa turned to gather up the few things that she thought she might need, including some coins, and then yelled across the house to the other children and told them that their dinner would be ready in about a half of an hour and that she would be back soon, and then she turned in a hurry to walk out of the front door.

Before reaching the front door, Robert asked, "Mom, are you going out into public dressed like that?" Robert was bewildered as he looked down at his mother in amusement, who was wearing what looked like a pair of men's trousers.

Melissa snapped back at her son hastily, "and what exactly is wrong with what I am wearing? I don't need to worry about fashion, nor do I need to wear a fancy dress, or any other costume for that matter in order to take care of my family. My little boy is sick, and he needs help. That is all that I have to care about. This is a real-life matter, son. And when it comes to these matters, I don't have any more time to worry about things like pretty little stupid dresses."

Robert replied sheepishly, "I just meant that you are going to be riding in public, and you know how it is in that city."

Melissa interrupted Robert's statement and cut him off sharply, "do you know what? I really don't care if I never wear another dress again. And I really do not care what anyone thinks of me! I have worked, and I have sacrificed, and I will wear whatever I want to. And from now on, if anyone has a problem with that, then that is exactly what it is- it is their problem!" Melissa turned to face her son and felt the heat rise in her cheeks as her upper lip snarled. Robert could hear her back teeth grinding, and he could see the tension and the strength pop out along her jawline as she clenched down and tightened her jaw muscles.

Robert explained softly, "Mom, I didn't mean to upset you. Of course, you can do whatever you want to. It's just that I've never seen you in a pair of men's trousers before. It is not common for a woman to wear pants, especially if the woman is attractive. And it is especially uncommon in that city. That's all."

Robert felt defeated. He had not meant to offend or upset his mother. He only wanted to protect her from anything that might harm her, including any harmful, negative, or judgmental comments that were likely to be made in society regarding her unusual and unconventional choice of clothing.

Melissa let out a deep sigh and then replied, "that's fine." Her words came out cold and flat. She did not want to argue with her son over her fashion choice, and time was passing by quickly as the evening sky was only becoming darker, and more ominous and more threatening.

Melissa took in a sharp breath and said, "I am thankful that you are looking out for me, Robert. But right now, we just need to get going. That's the reality. It is getting late, and it is getting dark very fast."

Melissa opened the door to the front of the house, stepped out onto the porch, and without a pause began to make her way over to a small corral that was used to pen up her horse.

Robert closed the door behind him and made sure that the children would be safe and secure in the house before making his way over to mount his horse. Robert's horse had been owned by the orchard farm for several years before Robert negotiated a deal for the animal. As soon as Robert took possession of the horse, he immediately put it into retirement and decided to rename it Yavapai. He rode Yavapai, but retirement meant that the horse was no longer used as a working animal for endless hours in the summer under the merciless desert sun.

Melissa had a black horse that she had raised from the time that it was a foal that she had named Scout. The little foal had earned its name when it was only a few minutes old, and it had wandered around and had chosen to scout the area and decided to cuddle up affectionately with Melissa rather than turning towards its own mother. Melissa climbed onto the grown animal and adjusted herself nervously in the saddle. When she was comfortable, Melissa looked over at Robert, who was already waiting patiently.

"We ready?" She asked of her firstborn son.

"Ready as we'll ever be. Follow me and stay close behind me. Dad gave me some specific instructions in regard to some things to be on the lookout for." Robert instructed his mother, remembering that his father had specifically stated that he would drop some of his tools at the crossing if he should happen to make it there before Melissa did.

"Alright," Melissa replied quizzically. "If that's what you want to do, let's do it."

Both of the horses turned and began to trot away from the house, carrying Melissa and Robert out and towards the road and the nearby camp where they were expecting to meet up with George.

Robert leaned over in his saddle towards Melissa and yelled out, "we are going to ride through the camp, and when we get to the road, I am going to look around a little bit. If I don't find anything, we can wait there. It's after twilight and the sun is getting low behind the mountains. It will be dark in no time now. Hopefully, Dad is making good time."

Melissa listened intently and did not respond immediately. She simply nodded her head in agreement and followed Robert towards the camp. It was a short distance, and it did not take long for the horses to carry Melissa and Robert to the intersection and the crossroads on the trail. When they reached the crossing in the road, Robert surveyed the area in search of his father's blacksmithing tongs. After searching and circling his horse several times, he told Melissa, "there's nothing."

Melissa looked at Robert with a puzzled expression and then asked, "what is that supposed to mean?"

Robert thought about it for a moment and then told his mother, "it means that Dad hasn't been here yet. More specifically, it means that he is still heading this way from Lynx Creek, and it means that we need to decide what the best course of action will be and what we are going to do from here. Basically, we need to decide if we are going to stay and wait for them here, or if we should start making our way towards them."

Melissa felt a wave of panic set in, and it was becoming increasingly more difficult with every passing moment for her to hold in her growing frustrations. Melissa's voice was high-pitched, and she spoke quickly, "we should head towards them and the cabin, of course."

"But wait," Robert interrupted. While he and his brothers were riding back to the house to get his mother, he had already considered the possibility, and he already decided that the rough conditions on the trail would make backtracking more challenging.

Robert continued, "I know that you're anxious and I know that you have the best of intentions, but if we wait for just a short amount of time, maybe only as much as fifteen minutes, Dad and Georgie will come right through here. They can pick up and run with us into the city from here. If we go back towards Lynx Creek, we will technically meet up with them a few minutes sooner, but that will make it more difficult for Dad to travel from there because the trails and the roads are washed out in quite a few places, and they are as bad as they have ever been. It is already going to be a hard ride for Dad being two-up. It would be too many horses to safely gallop and move up that trail with any amount of real speed."

Robert paused for a moment, sighed, and then continued, "plus, we still have to travel almost ten miles through these mountains just to get into Prescott. We need to take it easy on these horses with the trails and the roads being so bad because we still have quite some distance to cover. It doesn't help that we are going to have to do this ride in the dark, so we have to kind of mitigate all of our dangers from right here and right now."

Melissa would have preferred to have started heading south to meet up with George sooner. But waiting was a sensible and well-thought-out decision, even if she did not prefer it. Melissa felt comforted and safer because she was with Robert. The young man had grown up making practical, sensible, and rational decisions, and he knew the trails and the roads well enough to understand the best course of action. Melissa looked down as her hands fidgeted with the horse's reins and she quietly replied, "yeah, you're right. It is only going to get darker as the sun sets further, and we don't want to lose any precious time or useful daylight."

Robert watched as his mother fumbled, folded, and twisted a small section of the reigns around aimlessly. He could tell that she was nervous and frightened. As their oldest child, and after witnessing so many of his family's milestones in life, he knew exactly what each of his mother's expressions meant. Life had been difficult for them as early pioneers and miners in Yavapai County, and because the region was still in its youth respectively, it had been more difficult for them to manage and to cope with real-life events, such as when Melissa's mother had died just a year after George had moved with Melissa and their children to Arizona. Melissa had desperately wanted to take the 3-week train ride back to Quebec to be with her father as they both mourned the loss of her mother. However, between the costs, and the fact that it would require nearly two months' worth of time to travel and to make the roundtrip journey, Melissa decided that she simply could not make the trip back home. Instead, during the days surrounding her mother's funeral, she was at her home in Walker, and Robert watched on as his mother spent most of that time in tears.

There was no question that living and surviving in the rural region was more difficult for the pioneer miners and their families than it was for those that lived in larger cities and established their lives in close proximity to their extended family members. Robert witnessed the challenges again for himself earlier in the year when the smelters had closed, and the local economy was severely affected by widespread social and financial challenges. While the hardworking families in the new and rural areas struggled to get supplies, such as lumber, or food, life in the city had continued on almost as though nothing had happened.

Robert had also seen his parents in some of their most joyous moments, such as when his siblings were born, or when they had arrived in Prescott. Robert smiled in amusement as he remembered watching his mother's reaction to the new place. He could clearly remember how gentle and hopeful his mother's eyes looked after they had finally arrived in Prescott after the long journey. He remembered seeing the same look on Melissa's face after they had finalized the purchase of the little Walker house. Robert was proud of the special occasions, the celebrations, and their successes.

Having had enough of the silence and the waiting, Melissa grew impatient and asked Robert sharply, "what are his symptoms? Georgie's symptoms. What are they?"

Robert replied, "yeah, I knew what you meant. Well, honestly, he has a bad fever. Dad tried to get it down. He placed a cool rag over his forehead and along his neck, and he made sure that Georgie was drinking water. Dad said that he had done everything that he knew how to do to treat a fever. I guess the fever, or the illness just got progressively worse." Robert did his best to recollect everything that he observed about his little brother while he was inside of the cabin. He also remembered what his father told him about what should be revealed to Melissa regarding the little boy's condition.

Robert looked at his mother, shook his head, and said, "you know, there were a few things that just didn't seem right to me. But I don't know what to think about it because we were only back from work for a couple of minutes when Dad decided that we needed to get some help. So, I'm just not sure what to make of it all."

Robert selected his words carefully, and he was in a deep train of thought when the sound of a distant horse in a full gallop reached his ears. He looked up along the darkened trail and asked, "do you hear that? That is going to be them. That horse is coming in way too fast to be anyone else." Robert knew that anyone coming home from work would be in a hurry, but not in a running gallop kind of hurry.

Melissa and Robert adjusted their positions and made sure to keep their horses clear of the road in case George's fast-moving horse should miss a step. Only a few seconds passed by, and then Melissa recognized the shadowy image of George in the distance on his horse running north up the trail towards them. She extended her arm, pointed in her husbands general direction, and said to Robert, "there they are." Her words came out hollow and empty.

At that same moment, George spotted Melissa and Robert on the side of the road and quickly slowed his horse down to a trot. As George approached, Melissa and Robert each gave their horses a gentle squeeze and joined George as he passed by the crossing.

Melissa looked over at her husband, who was holding their son. She observed the shirt that George used as a makeshift sack that was cradling the boy. The growing darkness hindered the view, and Melissa could barely make out the boy's soft features.

Melissa's voice was shaky as she asked her husband, "George, what's going on with him? The boys came back, and they didn't tell me a lot about what is going on. They said that he had a fever and that he might have influenza. What is going on with him?"

Melissa waited several moments for George to answer, and she felt confused by the expression that she saw on George's face. It was a look that she had never seen her husband make before.

George looked at Melissa impatiently, and with an odd glare that shot an instant bolt of fear straight through to her core as he shouted, "I really don't know, Liz. Yes, he has a fever, and it is pretty high. He's been burning up for a while. But look, we need to get him some help now. Let's just get there, and then I can fill you in on every detail. Okay? It's serious enough that we need to go, now."

Melissa shouted back calmly, "Okay. Let's go. You lead. We will be right here behind you. Oh, and be careful."

George nodded his head and said firmly, "I'm going to do it."

George squeezed his legs hard, and his horse broke out into a fast gallop. Melissa and Robert followed immediately behind him.

Chapter 14

September 14th, 1899 - Prescott, Arizona

Most of the trails and most of the roads were rutted and washed out. Several trees had fallen and were blocking segments of the trail, making it difficult to pass in some places. The fallen trees combined with the steep terrain and deep, washed-out crevices, proved to be cumbersome for the horses. It was slow going as the midnight hour closed in and the darkness of the hour took ahold of the land, and it took much more time than usual to clear the distance.

Melissa was frustrated after navigating the difficult and weathered forest trails in the darkness, and she was eager to learn more about what was going on with her little son. It had been a difficult ride through the mountainside knowing that her son was suffering from an illness and that there was nothing that she could do, but ride. She felt a wave of relief when they finally made it off of the rugged mountain path and arrived in Prescott to find that the roads in the downtown area were well maintained.

The horses moved through the downtown area quickly, and they passed by the bars, the shops, the restaurants, and the hotels, at a fast and steady gallop. The horses slowed as they turned left onto Gurley Street, passing nearby the railroad station along the way. As they made the turn, they were completely oblivious to the townspeople that were still out and enjoying the mild summer weather and had mostly stopped in their places to watch the commotion and to see which direction the fast-moving horses were headed. It was not always a sign of trouble, but, more often than not, fast-moving horses in the downtown area of the city at that time of night, especially when it was within the vicinity of the Railroad Depot, it was a sign that either something bad had happened or that something bad was about to happen.

"There is less than a mile to go. Follow me around and through these curves and we will be there shortly." George shouted back over his shoulder to Melissa and Robert, both of whom were not far behind him.

The sound of the horses hooves echoed loudly off of the bungalows and the small farm homes that lined the street as they continued on their way towards the Sisters of Mercy hospital. The roads in the city were dark, but they were maintained well enough that it allowed for a quick and easy passage. Though they were near the Hospital, George began to struggle with the ride. He had kept his son in the shirt in front of him, and the long ride up through the mountain trails had put a lot of strain and stress on his neck and his back. George grimaced and winced from the searing pain, and then he pushed his horse harder. He pushed himself to remain focused on his task, and the only thing that mattered to him at that very moment was getting some help for his little boy.

The last half of a mile was the hardest stretch of the journey. George, Melissa, and Robert were each facing their own set of fears and unique set of emotions, and the stress from all of it was building up as they moved quickly by the last stretch of houses. They galloped passed the row of small farm homes that lined Grove Avenue, becoming more eager and more anxious to arrive at their destination after traveling the long distance. As the horses galloped quickly around and through the curve, Melissa had to blink back her tears when the hospital was finally within their sight.

The windmill and the water tower that were situated to the rear and to the left of the large hospital building stood hidden in the shadows behind the depths of the darkness. Melissa could not make out all of the details of the nearby pine trees, but she could make out their shapes and their general forms in the shadowy darkness. She drew in a deep breath, and she found that the fragrance from the pinion pines was sweet and calming. Though the darkness absorbed most the city, the cottonwood trees that lined the front of the hospital were visible, standing tall and thick, with heavy branches covered in silky, dark green leaves. Melissa was relieved to find that the walkway to the central office and the entry to the building were illuminated by gas lamps and were visible under the darkness of night.

The horses quickly slowed from a gallop to a trot as they approached the front of the building. Robert stopped his horse abruptly and dismounted the animal as fast as he could. Melissa managed to get her horse stopped quickly and dropped down from her horse only a moment after Robert had his feet on the ground. George brought his horse to a slow stop between them, and he looked down at his son swaddled in the large shirt that was pulled over the front of him.

Melissa took a few heavy steps towards George, who was still sitting on his horse. Melissa glared at George while he sat there motionless looking down on the little boy, and then she said, "Okay, George. We made it all the way here. Give him to me. Hand him down to me and tell me what's going on."

George ignored Melissa's impatient tone. Instead he focused on his son, and he moved slowly and cautiously as he began to pull on the sleeves of the shirt that he used to cradle the boy against him until the white fabric slipped down from his shoulders. He pulled at the material until it was off, and his arms were free.

Robert joined Melissa and stood tightly by her side, ready to help her in guiding the boy down. George was careful in the way that he held his son, and he pulled the little boy close to his chest and held onto him. He placed a kiss on the top of the boy's head before gently lifting the boy's legs up and over the horn of the saddle, and then he handed the boy who was still swaddled in the adult sized shirt down to Melissa and Robert.

Melissa extended her arms and grabbed a hold of her little son. Robert assisted in order to ensure that the child that was three-quarters of Melissa's size, was safely handed down into her arms.

Melissa grew alarmingly concerned when the little boy made no effort to grab onto Melissa or to hold onto her in return. As the little boy laid his cheek gently onto Melissa's left shoulder with his face pressed into his mother's neck, he began to cry silently. Melissa could feel the heat from his wet tears on her skin and she whispered, "it's okay, baby. I know. You have a really high fever. But it's going to be okay. Mama is here now. Mama's here."

Melissa rocked her son gently and stroked his smooth, dark hair as she tried to comfort him. Realizing that she still had responsibilities, she asked, "Robert, can you please tie up the horses for me? And then can you head inside and see if there is anyone awake and attending to the office? Let the sister or the registered nurse know that I am bringing him in and that I will be right in behind you."

Robert nodded his head vigorously in agreement. He quickly tied up the horses, took off his hat, and rushed to turn and make his way towards the entrance to the hospital. Melissa turned her focus back towards her ill son.

George was slow to make the dismount from his horse, and most of his focus was placed on Melissa as she nurtured the little boy. The moment that his feet hit the ground he felt the weight of the world fall onto his shoulders. He struggled to catch his breath and every muscle that he had burned inside of him. Somehow, he managed to keep himself together and he straightened himself up. He stretched his back, and then extended his hands out towards his wife and said flatly, "I can take him now, Liz."

Melissa replied confidently, "thanks, but I've got him." She had already decided that once she had the little boy in her arms that she was not going to let go of him, not until there was a nurse or a doctor available to see him. She would be the one that would carry her son into the hospital.

"Ready?" She asked, and without waiting for a response, she turned and started to walk towards the front of the hospital.

Though she was determined to carry him, the boy was heavy enough that Melissa was relieved to see that the walkway to the entrance of the hospital was relatively easy, with just a small staircase, and a short walk across a wooden patio to the front door. Melissa walked slowly and put all of her attention on making sure that the little boy suffered from as little discomfort as possible.

George caught up with her and then walked tightly by her side, guiding her along the way. When they reached the entrance, George opened the wooden entry door for his wife and his son. The heavy door let out a loud screech, and it thumped heavily when it closed behind them. From somewhere inside of the dimly lit office space they could hear a woman's voice followed by Robert's voice wafting in. They stood wide-eyed, waiting for a nun or a nurse, and for their son, Robert, to appear from somewhere within the building.

A nun, one of the sisters of mercy, spoke mostly to herself as she entered the room from a hallway and greeted George and Melissa. "Oh, they've already made it in. Good, good. Welcome to the Sister's of Mercy."

Robert followed closely behind the nun and watched as the sister pointed towards the young boy that was braced in Melissa's arms and asked, "this young gentleman just came in and told me that you were coming in with another young boy who is said to be quite ill. This is the young boy in question I take it?"

Melissa's face was pale, and her eyes flooded with tears as she replied, "yes, sister. He has a very high fever. He's burning up." Melissa could feel the heat from the boy's body radiating against hers, which caused her to break out into a cold, clammy sweat.

"I see." The sister replied calmly. "I am going to ask you to carry him back into an examination room. That is where we will be able to evaluate him."

"That will be great. Thank you, sister." Melissa replied weakly. They all echoed similar sentiments as Robert sat down in a chair that was placed quaintly beside the front door, and George and Melissa followed the sister down a long hallway and into a spacious examination room. There was an examination table and a physician's chair at the center of the room, and there were two small wooden chairs positioned on the left side of the bed. At the head of the bed there was a small porcelain washbasin that was attached to the wall.

As they entered the well-lit room, the sister turned towards Melissa and asked, "does he have any other symptoms, or is there anything else that is going on with him that I might need to know about?" The sister looked at Melissa and she slowly scrunched up her face while she waited for a response.

George scratched at the side of his head and smoothed out the side of his hair, and then he leaned forward as he replied on Melissa's behalf, "I was actually the one that was with him when he developed the fever. I am not sure if I can explain it, but he has a little fever rash or something going on, and he looked bloated. He just didn't seem to look right."

The sister tapped on the wooden examination table and told Melissa to, "lay him down here, please." The sister then looked back towards George and said, "you were saying that he has a fever, a rash, and bloating. Is there anything else that you might have noticed? For example, how has his appetite been?"

While the nun finished questioning George, Melissa placed the boy onto the surface of the hard examination table. Melissa attempted to shift the boy in order to make him more comfortable, causing the large shirt that George had placed over the boy to fall and to drop loosely onto the cold wood table beside the boy. The boy's shirt was still unbuttoned, and it also fell open to reveal his severely swollen abdomen. Under the light from the gas lamps, Melissa was finally able to take her first look at her son and his condition. She was shocked, startled, and terrified into silence by what she was observing. She felt an overwhelming sense of panic begin to wash over her as she waited for

George, or for the sister, or for anybody to say something that would make this illness with her son make some kind of sense to her.

The nun waited for a reply, but when she received no response, she washed her hands in the small washbasin, placed a surgical mask over her face, and then said, "those pink spots that you can see on his chest and neck, he has several of them that are close together or are connecting, which does cause them to appear similar to a fever rash. His abdomen is also swollen and very bloated. Has he been evacuating his bowels regularly?"

George and Melissa looked at one another, and both of them realized that they were not certain of the answer. George looked at the nurse and muttered, "well, sister, Ma'am, he did skip dinner the other night. But, other than that, I don't know about his- I don't know, I suppose that I can call it output. It's the end of the summer and he is getting ready to start school on Monday, so he's been with me for most of the week, and I haven't been keeping track of his evacuation habits."

The little boy interrupted the conversation between his father and the sister by letting out a dry, harsh cough. The sister's eyebrows raised to form two high peaks on her forehead at the sound of the cough, and then her eyes narrowed down over her mask as she peered down at the young boy's face. The sister looked up at George and Melissa, and she held up a stethoscope as she stated, "okay, I would like to listen to his lungs. I am going to use this, and I will just listen to the sounds that are being produced in there."

The sister placed the metal against the boy's chest, and the coldness of it made the little boy twitch. The sister then slid the chest piece and the diaphragm of the stethoscope over the little boy's belly. The little boy grimaced, groaned, and twitched in pain. She already had her suspicions about what was causing his ailments. Still, she wanted to complete her assessments and run a culture test before offering any diagnosis or prognosis. The sister spoke softly while she quietly made further observations regarding the boy's reaction to her touching his bloated and tender abdomen, "I'm very sorry, my sweet child. I just need to listen to what is going on inside of there for just a moment."

The sister pulled the stethoscope away from the boy, and then delicately closed his shirt over, leaving the buttons undone. The sister turned to look at Melissa and then at George, and said, "as a part of his evaluation, I would like to take his blood pressure, and his temperature, and then I suggest that we run a diagnostic test that uses a simple blood serum culture to check for possible bacteriological diseases."

George and Melissa looked at one another with lost, confused expressions. George finally turned to face the sister after he mustered up the courage to give a response, "yeah, sure. If you think that he needs it, then, of course, yes. Do it."

The sister pointed to the washbasin, the soap, and a short pile of brilliant white washcloths, and replied, "very good. You're welcome to stay here with your son as long as you would like to. We have water piped in, and because your son is quite ill and could be contagious, I am going to ask you both to wash your hands and to tend to your hygiene in order to ensure your cleanliness while I get a few things prepared."

After a moment of shuffling around the room, the sister left the room while promising to return with a few things so that she would be able to get an accurate reading of the young boy's vital signs, and so that she could take a blood sample. Melissa and George both sat quietly for some time, neither one of them knowing exactly what to say.

Melissa stared at her little boy lying on the examination table. His dark hair had grown in and had become quite long over the summer, and it was strewn across and stuck against his smooth forehead with perspiration. Melissa stared at her son and thought back to the day that she had given birth to him. She could see his perfect little toes and his full head of dark hair. She remembered how she had closed her eyes and kissed the newborn baby gently on the top of his head.

In her memory, as she opened her eyes, the baby suddenly aged and was two years old. Melissa could see the toddler jumping down from her arms and sprinting across the front yard, and then he jumped into the arms of his father. Melissa smiled and waved at her son. The boy waved back at his mother and moved his hand quickly in front of his face, creating a blur.

When the boy dropped his hand, he was suddenly five years old. How he smiled on that day. It was the day that his first baby tooth fell out. He held his hand out towards his mother, proudly smiling at the tooth that was cradled in his tiny hand. Melissa watched and laughed at her son, who was adamant in telling her that she needed to "look closer" to see his new incoming adult tooth. Melissa looked closely and zoomed in to focus on the tiny adult tooth buds that were peeking through his soft pink gumline.

When Melissa pulled her focus back away from her son's lost tooth, the little boy was suddenly sitting at the dining room table, at the center of his family. There was a cake on the table that was topped with eight light blue candles that were glowing, and the little boy let out a roar of a laugh as his father teased him about becoming an old man on his eighth birthday.

The nun reentered the room abruptly, and the noise stirred Melissa from her memories. The nun looked directly at Melissa and then stated gently, "I'm sorry, but your son is very ill, and after I am finished collecting all of the data for his tests and assessments, I am going to get him dressed in a hospital gown and then we will move him to a room where we will be able to help him to relax and to recover comfortably. For his tests, you are welcome to remain in the room if you would like. It should take about one minute to take the blood pressure, and it will only take about five minutes to get an accurate reading of his temperature. The blood draw takes less than a minute to get enough of a sample to run the culture, and the downside to the blood draw is that it is a little painful." The sister waited for a moment, smiled softly behind her mask, and then added, "just a little."

Melissa took a deep breath and proclaimed, "I'm staying." George nodded his head, and then said flatly, "me too. But then I'm going to need to go and find Robert and tell him that he should ride back into the downtown area of the city and get us all a hotel room since it sounds like we are going to be here for a while."

Chapter 15

September 14th, 1899 - Prescott, Arizona

Little George was moved into a room with a large window and a view that overlooked the road below. The room had a bed, two chairs, a table, and a porcelain washbasin that was affixed to the wall in the far-left corner of the room. There were two gas lamps in the room, and both were casting a soft glow, as well as long, shadowy figures across the floor.

Melissa and George had walked around the room and stared out of the window into the darkness of night, muttering and mumbling about George's temperature reading being at 104.2 degrees Fahrenheit. The sister explained that the high-grade fever was a defense mechanism, and then suggested that she would try giving the boy an amount of Dover's powder. She went on to suggest that they could try to use a new drug that was available called salicylates, or aspirin, and along with the Dover's powder, it might also help to reduce his fever. When the sister was certain that George and Melissa understood what was happening with their little boy, she calmly explained that they would need to remain isolated in the hospital room with their son until after they received the results of their son's blood culture test.

Several hours had passed since the sister took the blood culture and administered some of the medications. Melissa stood beside the window and watched as the first light from the sunrise brought in a brilliant, bright red light that crested and grew along the eastern mountain horizon. She was amazed by the lingering clouds that picked up tones of raspberry pinks and soft lilacs that grew and stretched westward with the rising sun. Melissa looked down towards the street and noticed that the road below was dark and still under the cover of the last of the night's shadows. It would not be long before the hustle and bustle of city life would start moving around and making noise on the streets below them.

Little George slept through most of the night, and as the morning sun began to filter into the room, the boy began to stir. He looked over and saw his mother standing beside the window. Then he looked towards the side of the bed and at his father and said, "Dad." His little voice was gravelly and hoarse, but he continued, "I was dreaming, and in my dream, I found a lot of gold. I found it, and it wasn't where I thought it would be. It wasn't at the Lynx Creek cabin, Dad. I found it at home. It was at home, in Walker." George stood up and moved close to the side of the little boy's bed as the little boy coughed and wheezed.

George leaned in and smiled brightly at his son, and then replied, "well, that sounds like it was a pretty good dream, son."

George used two of his fingers to gently wipe the hair back and off of his son's forehead. He smiled brightly again and then said to his son, "for now, you just need to lay here and get well, and then we can make that dream happen. We are going to find that gold." George continued smiling at his little boy.

The little boy scanned the hospital room, revealing that the white of his eyes had become a solid blood red. George noticed that the little boy looked old, weak, and tired. His young face appeared to have rapidly aged with the illness. George became concerned as the sun rose along the horizon and was high enough to flood the room with daylight, and he noticed that his son's skin had taken on an unusual yellow color.

"Dad, I don't feel good. I don't want to stay here anymore. Can we please just go back home or to the cabin? I just want to go home." The little boy pleaded.

Melissa smiled from where she stood beside the window and then added her thoughts, "Georgie, those are two different places. What about me? Do you want to go to the cabin, or do you want to go home with me?"

The little boy smiled, closed his eyes, and said, "I want to look for gold at home, and then I want to go to the cabin, mama. I love being at the cabin. But I want you to go to the cabin with me because you're my favorite of all."

George laughed and then smiled tenderly as he looked down at his little boy and said, "first we need to get you back to being healthy, and then we can do whatever it is that you want to do. If you want to go home, we will take you home. If you want to go to the cabin, we will take you to the cabin. But we need you to get better first, son."

Little George coughed a long, dry cough, and mumbled, "I just want to go home now. I'm sorry that I got sick, Dad. I didn't mean to."

George smiled a sad little smile and said, "don't think about it like that, son. This is not your fault. We are going to get you back to being healthy, and everything is going to be okay. You'll be home in a day or two, and then you'll be busy starting school."

The little boy looked up at his father through hazy, glossy eyes, and sighed heavily before he spoke, "it doesn't matter, Dad. I just want to go home with you and mom. That's all." As soon as he was done speaking, the boy closed his eyes and he quietly drifted off to sleep.

George sat down and sat back in his seat. He was distraught with worry. Melissa looked at her husband and then quietly walked across the small room to sit down beside him. Melissa fidgeted with her shirt sleeves out of nervousness. After only a moment passed, they turned to face one another, and without saying a word, George extended his arms and pulled his wife into a hug. He held her there for a moment, and then he heard the unsteady rhythm in her breathing, and he recognized the soft heaving convulsions in her shoulders. It only took a moment for him to realize that she was crying. George knew that Melissa's heart was breaking because his heart was breaking too.

They held onto one another for quite a while, and eventually pulled apart, dried their eyes, and turned their attention and shifted their focus towards the anticipation of seeing a doctor and receiving the diagnostic test results.

"It shouldn't be too much longer." Melissa eventually stated in an impatient tone. "Last night, the nun said that the doctor makes his visits first thing in the mornings. And it's morning."

"Yes. She did, and it is." George smirked at his wife as he spoke. He had always loved her feisty nature. His smirk shifted to a thin, flat smile as he continued, "they'll be around soon, Liz. It's still pretty early yet."

Melissa sighed heavily and said, "I know that it is still quite early. But we have been waiting and waiting. It feels like we have been waiting forever." Melissa leaned her head over onto her husband's shoulder and closed her eyes. George leaned his head back gently to rest his head against the side of Melissa's head and closed his eyes.

Neither Melissa nor George had slept since they had arrived in the city, and in the calmness and quietness of the sunrise, they both accidentally dozed off and fell asleep. After only a little more than a half an hour of resting, they were abruptly woken and startled by the noise of the registered nurse, who entered the room while shouting loudly, "the doctor is on the premises, and he will be around to make his visits shortly. Please be prepared with any questions or concerns that you might have."

Melissa and George both sat upright quickly and tried to shake off their exhaustion. Melissa interjected before the nurse could leave, "but wait, please. Hold on, because I am confused, and I don't seem to understand. We haven't received the results from my son's evaluation, or from his blood test yet."

The nurse waited for a moment, looked Melissa up and down, paused to look at her trousers before making eye contact with her, and then returned her gaze as she stated in an almost sarcastic tone, "that would be a good question to ask the doctor, wouldn't it?"

The nurse waited for several moments, and when neither George nor Melissa had anything more to say to her, she silently turned on her heel and walked out of the room just as abruptly as she had entered it.

George stretched his arms above his head, yawned loudly, and then asked, "what do you think all of that unnecessary noise was all about?"

"I don't know." Melissa replied and then said, "I want to accuse her of being rude because of the way that she looked at my clothes. But I think that her problem is based on the fact that they just want to ensure that everyone is awake and at full attention when the doctor is making his rounds so that everyone gets the answers that they are looking for as quickly as possible. After all, they have a lot of other patient rooms to manage as well as ours. There are a lot of sick people here, and everyone wants their answers, just like we do."

George gave Melissa a smile, yawned, and then said, "that's true. See, and here I was thinking that maybe it was that she was being rude because she is rude." George smirked and shook his head from side to side and then confessed, "I forgot how many rooms they have here. You're probably right. They just want everyone to be ready and prepared to speak with the doctor so that they can stay on a schedule. And you just proved where little Georgie got all of his brains. His mama."

Melissa gave George the side-eye, and then looked down towards the wooden polished floor and smiled the saddest smile that George had ever seen. George knew that there was nothing that he could possibly say that would make her feel any better, mostly because he already understood that there was not anything that anybody could say that would make him feel any better under the given set of circumstances.

Melissa sat upright, used her slender fingers to smooth out her hair, and then straightened out her blouse. She became quite restless and had to force herself to calm down and to sit still as they waited for the doctor to visit their son in the hospital room. She looked at her little boy sleeping on the bed peacefully, and just watched him as she let the minutes pass by. George looked on at the boy, and he sat quietly even though he wanted to share his concerns and the fear that he was feeling.

In time, the doctor finally gave a short knock on the door and then pushed the door open and entered the room. "Good morning, I am Doctor Robinson." The doctor stated as he entered the room and glanced at Melissa, looking specifically at her trousers before making solid eye contact with her, and then allowed the door to gently close behind him as he stated confidently, "it is my pleasure to meet you, Ma'am."

"Likewise. It's nice to meet you, doctor." Melissa smiled gently and nodded politely as she greeted the doctor.

George stood up and extended his hand towards the doctor. The doctor looked at George very squarely, and then took George's hand and shook it firmly. As they shook hands, George said, "it is my pleasure to meet you, sir. You have to forgive our appearance. We made the emergency trip into the city last night, and neither of us has had the opportunity to do much of anything, least of all make ourselves presentable."

"Oh, you're perfectly fine. There is nothing wrong with either one of you." The doctor stated as he smiled a thin, genuine smile, and then walked to the side of the bed and looked down at the little boy. Rather than putting the child through any unnecessary discomfort, the doctor opted to observe the boy while allowing him to stay comfortably asleep. The doctor tilted his head as he made a few observations about the boy. He could see the boy's severely bloated abdomen, and he knew that it was likely that the child's colon was distended.

After several moments passed, the doctor straightened himself up, and then he turned to face George and Melissa. He let out a soft sigh and then said, "there really is no easy way for me to tell you this, so I am just going to come right out with it, and I will get straight to the point. Your son's blood culture came back positive for a bacterial infection called enteric fever. You may or may not be familiar with the term, but it is more commonly referred to and is more widely known as typhoid fever."

As soon as the doctor finished stating the diagnosis, Melissa burst out into tears. She leaned into George, burying her face into his pant leg, and tried her best to stifle and quiet her sobs.

The doctor continued, "I don't know how much you know about it, but typhoid fever is an extremely complicated matter. It is essentially a multisystemic disruption caused by bacterial toxicity."

The doctor paused for a moment and looked at George. He took a quick and sharp breath, and then attempted to explain it again, "basically, your son has a bacterial infection, and that is what is causing all of his symptoms, including causing his temperature to become so dangerously high. The treatment that he has already been given appears to have had little to no significant effect. His face appears yellow because typhoid causes liver problems, and the yellowness that you are seeing is because he has developed jaundice, which is associated with the liver problems. His eyes would probably also look yellow from it, except typhoid causes the eyes to become severely bloodshot, so this is what we are seeing instead of the yellowing. The disease is affecting multiple internal organs and their systems."

The doctor took a short breath and looked carefully at George and then at Melissa to make sure that they were still following his words. When he was certain that they were ready to hear more, he continued, "I do not want you to become any more concerned than you already are, but I must disclose to you that things could get worse. Your son is already displaying several different symptoms of the disease, and there is no way to know when new symptoms might appear. He could still suffer from confusion, delusions, delirium, or some other form of psychosis. He could suffer from cardiac problems, or possibly internal bleeding."

The doctor paused and pointed to the pink spot on the boy's cheek. "The rose or salmon-colored spots that appear on his neck, chest, and back in clusters or patches, these spots are also a symptom that is associated with typhoid fever. However, right now, what we need to be mostly concerned about is his abdomen, which is obviously severely bloated. The bloating is an indication that his colon is distended, and if it should worsen and if it should cause his intestine to become perforated it would require a surgical operation so that the perforation might be found and sutured."

The doctor stood up straight, and looked at George and continued, "the nurse wrote in his chart that he has not been eating or taking in any fluids on his own, so we will begin to give him intravenous fluids, and we will continue to give him the Dover's powder and also the salicylic acid. We will continue to monitor his temperature and his other vital signs, and we will monitor him for any other changes. Unfortunately, there is not much more that we can do. We simply need to wait. It probably wouldn't hurt to hope and pray that his immune system is strong enough to fight it."

George stood completely frozen in place as he took in the meanings of all of the words as they left the doctor's mouth. He understood the diagnosis very well. George remembered reading a story that was printed in a newspaper back in 1890, after a water pipe in Toronto had broken and the water supply became contaminated, and the result was a widespread typhoid endemic. The disease had spread quickly, and around 30 percent of the people that became infected with the bacterial disease died from it.

George was in shock. He tried to process everything that the doctor said, and then asked somberly, "so, what I hear you saying is that there is not anything else that you can do. Is that right? Is that the bottom-line behind what I'm hearing?" His wide, piercing blue eyes begged the doctor to do something more for his little boy.

The doctor looked over the top of his glasses at George and said calmly, "unfortunately, we just cannot do much more for him. What we have already done is what we can realistically do for him. We are giving him the fluids to try to keep him hydrated, and we will continue to try to bring his fever down. We will continue to monitor his vital signs for any changes, and we will continue to make him as comfortable as possible. Unfortunately, that is all that we can do. He is quite ill, sir. I am deeply sorry that I didn't have better news to bring to you."

Melissa steadied herself and pulled her face away from George's pant leg and looked over at her precious little boy sleeping soundly. Her fist was still grappling at George's pant leg, but she faced the doctor, drew in a sharp breath, and then stuttered and stammered, "but, what about, I mean, he's not going to get any worse, is he? You just said that it might get worse with more symptoms. But then he's going to get better. I mean, he is going to get better, right? Doctor?" Melissa's eyes were glazed, sunken, and hidden behind dark circles.

The doctor stated confidently, "Ma'am, I can only tell you that he is incredibly ill and that he has a bad infection in his gastrointestinal system and in his bloodstream, and his body or his immune system needs to fight it. Right now we just need to hope that he starts to respond to the medicine and that he starts to improve very, very soon."

Melissa did not know what to make of the response. Though she was not entirely satisfied with the reply, she looked over at her little boy and decided to accept the doctor's response as the reality. George had been watching the doctor closely and recognized that at the end of the doctor's statement, the angle at the inner corner of his eyebrows had changed. George immediately recognized the expression that briefly crossed the doctor's face, and he knew what he saw. It was genuine and authentic sadness.

George looked down at his wife, and then over towards his little son. He looked back at the doctor, and his heart sank. He knew what he saw, and he also understood what it implied. Because of the menacing illness, and because the treatments were not working, his little boy was in a particularly perilous and life-threatening state. George recognized that his son was in danger, and at that moment he was simply thankful that Melissa was distracted and happened to miss the changes in the doctor's facial expressions.

George put all of his effort into focusing on getting through the rest of the difficult conversation. He locked his eyes with the doctor and said slowly, "I understand, Doctor. Thank you, for taking care of my little boy."

The doctor looked directly at George and then said softly, "I promise that we will do everything that we can do for him." George nodded his head in agreement and gave the doctor a weak attempt at a smile.

The doctor looked back at George and gave him a gentle smile, and then said, "not that this is not enough for you to have to deal with, but you should know that typhoid is a highly infectious disease, which is why your son has been isolated in this room. This hospital has a small ward, and there are twenty-three other rooms that generally have either two or four people in them, but when there is the possibility of spreading a communicable or infectious disease through close contact, then a quarantine is required. I advise you to keep yourself and any of your family members that may have been exposed to the illness in isolation. I further advise you to remain in isolation until after your son's symptoms subside, or until you are certain that you and your other family members that might have been exposed to it are not infected with it."

George took a deep breath and let out a long sigh, and then replied anxiously, "we don't even know how this happened. I mean, this disease came from somewhere. It didn't just randomly occur."

The doctor nodded and affirmed, "you're correct. It occurs by consuming food or water that has become contaminated with the bacteria, or by coming into close contact with someone else that is either carrying the bacteria or is infected with the disease. Unfortunately, there is simply no way to test or to determine exactly what was responsible for causing your son to contract the illness. That being said, since you and your wife are not showing any symptoms of illness, and since you have not suggested that any of your other family members might be infected with it, it likely started with an isolated contaminated food source or an isolated contaminated water source."

George took a moment to think about it and went through all of the different possibilities that might have occurred and might have caused his little boy's illness. He thought back to when they had bought fresh corn from the market. He thought about the monsoon season, and the rainwater, and he remembered how hard it had been to get any water to come out of the defective and failing well in town. He tried to recall all of the different ways that his son might have come into contact with the bacteria.

George eventually realized that it did not matter where it came from. Instead, George accepted the reality and decided that the only thing that he could do was to focus on how they would need to clean the house and the cabin in order to remove the source of the contamination. The house and the cabin were going to need to be deep cleaned, and some specific items, such as George's bedroll, and little George's bed, would need to be burned and destroyed. George already understood that it was going to be necessary to discard everything within their food storage. Most importantly, he would need to replace all of the containers that he used to collect and store their drinking water.

After a moment of silence, the doctor said, "I hope that I have explained everything well enough for both of you to understand. Now, do either of you have any more questions or concerns that I can address for you today?"

George looked down at Melissa, who was still clinging to his trousers and shaking her head from side to side to answer the question with a no. George made solid eye contact with the doctor and replied quaintly, "no, sir. I don't believe that we do."

When the doctor was certain that neither George nor Melissa had any further questions, he looked back at the boy one more time, and then chose his words carefully so as not to upset the boy's parents, and he said, "I will be back around tomorrow. Rest well, son."

The doctor then tipped his head towards Melissa and then towards George, said a quick and courteous goodbye, and then took his leave.

Chapter 16
September 14th, 1899 - Prescott, Arizona

Robert stared at the wind-up clock that was perched on top of the bulky wooden nightstand. He had hoped that his mother or his father would have called for him, or that they would have joined him at the hotel by noon. He had spent most of the morning pacing the small room, and he was completely consumed with concern over his little brother. He was restless, and his restlessness was growing with every passing moment.

Robert was absolutely exhausted, but he could not bear the thought of sitting around and doing nothing when he knew that his brother was in trouble. When the hands of the clock turned to read 3:00pm, he decided that he would no longer sit and wait, and that he would not continue to aimlessly pace the floor for one more second. He hastily grabbed a few things from a round wood table and shoved them into his pocket before he bolted from the small room. He quickly made his way down a wooden staircase and then pushed through a thin crowd that was on the ground floor of the hotel lobby.

He took a long, deep breath when he made it into the outside air, and he hurried to reach his horse and untied it from the hitching post as quickly as he could. As soon as Robert mounted the saddle, he had his horse turned facing west on Gurley Street, and he gave the horse a quick, hard squeeze with his legs, and the horse broke out into a fast gallop. He rode fast as the horse took the turn to the north easily and was consistent and well balanced through the westward turning curves, and it only took a short amount of time to reach Grove Avenue.

As Robert approached the hospital, he looked towards the front of the building and was nearly astounded to find that his mother and father were exiting the front of the hospital just as he was arriving. His parents were walking tightly together, and both were looking downward towards the ground.

Robert pulled back on the reins of his horse and brought the animal to a stop about one hundred yards short of the hospital, and then focused his full attention on his mother and father. He could see that George was holding tightly onto Melissa's arm as they cautiously walked together down the wooden steps. At the bottom of the short staircase, George continued to hold onto Melissa's arm as they both slowly turned and moved towards their horses.

Robert watched his parents curiously, and he was struck by sheer terror when Melissa suddenly threw her head back and the most piercing and deafening scream that he had ever heard erupted from her lips.

"Why?" Melissa shrieked as she jerked and yanked her arm away from her husband's grasp. She thrust her hands upwards into the air, her long, thin fingers extended outward, and she screamed again, "why? Oh, God! Why?" As the shrill of the scream peaked in pitch and volume, Melissa's hands balled up into tightly clenched fists.

Robert could hear both grief and rage in her voice as his mother continued to scream, "why? Why my little boy?"

George felt defeated as he listened to his wife's screams. His eyes flooded with tears, and he struggled to breathe. George did everything that he could to focus on doing what he needed to do, which was to get Melissa calmed down enough to leave the front of the hospital. George reached out to his wife and pulled her towards him by the waist.

Melissa pushed back against her husband, and she flailed wildly against him in an attempt to get him to release her from his grip as she grunted, "No! You, let me go!"

George held onto his wife tightly as the tears streamed down her twisted face, and then he said softly, "woah, baby. It's okay. I know."

George knew that it would only take a few short moments before Melissa would run out of that highly charged energy, and the struggle would be over. And he was right. After about twenty seconds of thrashing, Melissa's struggling became less violent and less effective, and eventually, having spent the last of her energy, she collapsed into George's arms and sobbed heavily. George pulled his wife firmly into his arms, to both hold her and to support her. George buried his face in his wife's hair, and the tears began to flow freely from his eyes.

Melissa sobbed, and quietly whimpered, "it's not fair. It's just not fair. I don't know how to do this. He is my baby, and this is the wrong order. I'm supposed to die before any of them. I am not supposed to have to bury my child! It's just not fair."

Robert felt his stomach drop as he watched his mother and his father from a distance. He was not positioned close enough to hear what his mother was saying. However, he knew from watching their behavior that whatever had gone wrong with his little brother, it had gone very wrong. Robert used his legs and gave his horse a gentle, little squeeze, and the big animal slowly trotted towards George and Melissa. Robert stopped the horse a few feet away from where his mother and father were standing together as their entire world fell apart.

Robert allowed a few seconds to pass before he asked in an unwavering voice, "Dad? What happened?"

George snapped his head in surprise and looked up at his oldest son. George's bright, brilliant blue eyes were wide with shock, and suddenly they squinted down and his face became twisted with raw grief. He opened his mouth to talk, but no sound came out. Instead, he could only shake his head from side to side while Melissa continued to sob heavily on his shoulder.

Robert felt the sting of hot tears well up in his eyes as the realization of what happened set in. He was exhausted, he was confused, and he was heartbroken. Robert took a deep breath, and then made the dismount from his horse. Then, he turned and placed his arms around his mother and his father and embraced them as they cried.

He didn't know how much time had passed, but eventually, Robert pulled back from the hug and suggested, "I know that this is a lot to take in and we have a lot to deal with right now, but it would probably be better if we got off of the street and if we start heading back to the hotel. Is there anything else that you, or we need to accomplish while we are here?"

George shook his head to indicate that the answer was no. He swallowed hard and took a shaky, deep breath, and then told his oldest son, "we already had to sign all of the paperwork. Your brother, he is going to be buried," George paused and choked down a sob before he continued, "in the Citizens Cemetery, on the 18th. On Monday morning." George thought about how his son should have been starting school that same Monday morning, and his vision became blurred through thick and heavy tears.

Hearing his father say the words out loud, that his brother was going to be buried and that the funeral services were already scheduled, it caused Robert's heart to sink. Robert had never for a moment considered that his little brother might not make it through the illness. Robert could hardly believe it, and his heart was absolutely broken. He did not want to accept it, but there was nothing else that he could do.

Little George was gone.

Chapter 17

October 25th, 1899 - Lynx Creek, Arizona

Before George made his departure from the house that morning, he made the decision to take the morning off from work in order to visit the downtown area, specifically to visit the train station. He was waiting for a delivery, and he had already taken his horse and pulled his two-wheeled cart into town twice the week before to see if the package had arrived.

Waiting on the delivery had only added to the inner conflict and the anxiety that George had been feeling. He wanted the package to arrive, but he also didn't want to have to think about the package arriving. The delivery was important, and it mattered a great deal to him. So little had mattered to George lately, with the exception being Melissa and his children, and at least this was something that mattered.

When George arrived at the train station, he was surprised to find that the small downtown area was bustling. Between the market and the arrivals from the morning train lines, a considerable number of people were moving around, and they were making a considerable amount of noise. It was a warm afternoon, and though the first signs of winter were already beginning to set in across the high country, the mild autumn temperatures drew people out of their homes to shop and socialize in the quaint downtown area.

George waited and stood beside his horse, and he listened to the people talking as they moved along. He overheard one lanky, middle-aged gentleman telling another, shorter, more portly man that the roads going into Prescott had finally been repaired and that the city had just completed the addition of a brand-new sewer system. The shorter of the two men then commented that the road improvements would make the ride easier on Thursday to get some pears from the last carload of the season. The men moved on, and George shuffled his feet in frustration as he thought about the new sanitation system. He looked around in an attempt to find something else to focus on.

Only a moment passed when he overheard another man behind him, stating in a deep voice that the newspaper that very morning had announced that most of the mines were going to reopen after the courts agreed to relieve them of their debts. The man went on to suggest that the bigger news was that they were not going to be held financially responsible for any of the liabilities and labor accidents on any of the mining claims.

George listened and gently closed his eyes. He knew that it would be difficult in town, facing his neighbors and his peers, listening to them discussing the daily news and turning everything into trivial topics, all of them going on about their daily lives as though everything was fine while everything that was going on around him was a reminder that his little boy was gone. It was a devastating loss that he was still learning to live with, and the clamor around him was slowly destroying him at his core.

Hearing the men talk about the new sewer system and the mine liability relief, George could not help but to think about how badly Melissa had wanted to buy a house in Prescott because the city was modern, and many of the homes had water service and sanitation or sewer systems. George thought to himself that if he had only bought the house that Melissa wanted, everything might have been different, and little George might still be alive.

The news about the mining problems did not surprise him. The mining companies were often not held accountable for the accidents that happened. George understood that they were relieved of their overwhelming debts so that they could free up their cash flows and cover their operating expenses, and this would allow them to begin their operations again. However, there was a purpose behind the debt, and the debt relief felt like an insult to the miners that were on their feet day after day performing the hard labor, and they were all paying for it with their health. It was an even larger insult to the families whose loved ones had paid for it with their lives and were already waiting for the mining companies to provide them with a death benefit.

George took a slow, deep breath, and then reopened his eyes. He was beginning to perspire lightly underneath the warmth of the autumn sun. He took a handkerchief from his pocket and wiped his face with the clean white cloth. When he was satisfied that his face was presentable, he carefully folded the cloth and returned it to his pocket. He decided then that he had waited long enough, and that it was time to check on the status of his special delivery.

George turned impatiently and hurried to enter the railroad station. He found the small window to the rear and the left of the room in a wall that had a sign above it that read, "Shipping and Receiving." A short, white-haired man with thick spectacles perched on his bulbous nose sat behind the window, looking down at a short stack of paperwork. George recognized the man but, he could not recall the man's name. George was apprehensive, but he approached the window and addressed the man.

"Good day, sir. I am expecting a package, from the, uh, the Chicago Line." George stammered slightly as he spoke, but the old man at the window did not seem to notice it.

The old man looked up at George and said, "well, the Chicago line arrived a while ago. What is the name on the package?"

"Henderson. Mr. G.G. Henderson." George replied quaintly.

The old man smiled and replied politely, "okay, sure. I should have known that given that everyone knows who everyone is in these small towns. Mr. George Henderson, let me just take a look." The old man spoke as he reached across his desk and found another form, and then he scanned the information on the page and then said, "ah, yes. Here it is. We have it. It arrived this morning at just three minutes after ten o'clock. Let me get it for you. Please, wait here, sir. I'll be right back."

The portly old man grunted as he climbed off of his stool and walked towards another room located at the back of his office. "I'll just be a minute." George heard the old man say as he disappeared into the room at the rear.

George nodded politely and replied, "that's fine. Thanks." As the man disappeared into the backroom, George turned to scan the space inside of the train station. He had been in the station a countless number of times, but today the station looked different to him somehow. It seemed much smaller and much older than it had appeared just a few weeks prior. The aging wood and the darkened corners that once felt comfortable suddenly seemed foreign and unfamiliar. He couldn't help but to think that the old wooden building needed to be demolished and rebuilt. George rolled his eyes and then mumbled to himself, "maybe the problem is me. Maybe the building is fine, and maybe I am just getting to be too old."

George looked back towards the service window just in time to see the old man emerge from out of the shadowy darkness at the rear of the room. As the old man approached the counter, he said in a hoarsely strained voice, "here it is, sir. I do not know what's in here, but whatever it is, it's pretty heavy. You wouldn't happen to be in the lead market, would you sir?" The man said teasingly.

George raised his eyebrows and glared sharply at the old man. George was forced to remind himself that the man did not know anything about his life or his misery and that it was an innocent comment that if it had been made under any other circumstances, George would have given the comment a hearty laugh. George made his greatest effort to smile at the man's attempt at humor.

The man placed the pale wooden crate on the ledge of the counter, and then he looked down at the register sitting on his desk and stamped the paper next to the name G. G. Henderson, marking it with black ink as "received." The man looked back up at George, who was carefully taking the crate into his hands. The man thought to himself that it was odd how carefully George handled the package. It was almost as though the very act of touching the heavy box might cause it to crumble right in front of his very eyes.

George held the wooden box in his hands and thought that it was heavier than he had imagined that it would be. He looked up at the old white-haired man, who was observing him curiously and then said, "I really appreciate you handling this for me. Thank you, Sir." George nodded to the man, and then turned away abruptly and began walking swiftly towards the exit at the front of the train station.

George was so involved in his activities that he had not noticed the aging Mr. Miller, who was sitting on a bench across the station. Mr. Miller had recently heard the sad and shocking news about George and Melissa's little boy, and he thought that he might address George when he took notice of him. However, something about George's mannerisms and his appearance had caused Mr. Miller to allow the moment to pass, and instead, he watched as a dispirited version of the George that he knew took the package and left the station in a trance-like state.

Seeing George in that condition sent a wave of concern over Mr. Miller, and he made the decision at that moment to ride with his party back towards one of his homesteads in Lynx Creek, and then he would continue on alone from that point to Walker, to call on Melissa and George, in order to express his deepest condolences and sympathies. After all, they had been neighbors for some time, and the Henderson family had a particularly good reputation, and they were well liked within their community. George was one of the most well-known figures within Yavapai County, and he was known for being friendly, confident, reliable, and respectable, and all of his children were well known for being helpful, intelligent, and talented. Mr. Miller hung his head and realized in that moment that the sudden loss of the little Henderson boy was a loss that was going to be deeply felt and shared across the wider community.

George stepped out into the sunlight and carried the crate carefully. He approached his cart cautiously, and then placed the crate gently onto the cart behind the horse. He considered carrying the package in his arms in order to guarantee its safety, but from the moment that he picked it up he knew that it would simply be too heavy to carry. Instead, he looked down at the crate and adjusted its position, carefully placing it directly over the axels, guaranteeing that it would be safe on the cart during the short journey back to the cabin.

Chapter 18
October 25th, 1899 - Lynx Creek, Arizona

The ride back to the cabin should have been easy, but George was distracted by his thoughts, which made the trip longer and harder. The roads were clear, but there were a few small areas of washed-out ruts that George was required to pay special attention to along the trails headed back to the cabin. When the cart seemed unstable, George was relieved when he looked back over his shoulder to find that the crate was perfectly fine.

Silver came to a slow stop in front of the cabin. George looked down at his horse and let out a long and heavy sigh. He was slow to make the dismount, but he forced himself to get off of the horse and to find his footing on the ground underneath him. He tied the reins of the horse to the hitching post and then turned his attention towards the cart. George stopped short of picking the crate up. He simply stood there and stared down at it as though the crate was staring right back at him. He clenched his teeth tightly, allowing the muscles along his jawline to tighten and to bulge.

George wanted to pick up the package and carry it inside of the cabin, but he just could not do it. He was tired, and he just needed a little time to collect himself and to organize his thoughts. He decided that he would leave the crate on the cart. He reached for a shaft rest that was nearby the hitching post, and then disconnected the cart and moved it by hand, pushing and tugging it around until the shaft of the cart was immediately above the shaft rest. The cart was heavy and the task of moving it by hand was laborious.

"Silver," George said to his trusted horse as he struggled to catch his breath. With the cart positioned safely on the shaft rest, he moved to the side of his horse and stroked the horse's soft and silver colored, shiny mane and continued, "thanks for carrying that heavy thing for me, buddy."

He smiled at the large animal and gave it a gentle pat on its head before turning and walking away. He walked quickly towards his outdoor workshop and the forge that he had set up behind the cabin. He decided that he would focus on his work until he was ready to open the crate. His work had always been there to help to see him through.

He started a fire and planned to hammer out some iron bedsteads for the new electrical company in Walker, and some square-headed nails that another new homesteader in the area had personally asked him to hammer out two weeks prior. It was a beneficial project for George since he also needed several nails that would be useful towards making some repairs to the cabin, which was dilapidating a little more with every passing day.

George fired the square wrought iron, and then he placed it onto his anvil. He hammered the squared metal until the body was rounded and the end of the rod formed a sharp tip. George then took the rod and fired it again, heating it enough to cut off the sharpened tip. With the hammered metal still hot, George used a set of tongs to place the small, pointed, and rounded rod onto the anvil, and hammered the heated and softened metal until a head was formed on the top of the rod, forming a nail. George repeated this process over and over again, for hours.

George was not aware of how quickly time was passing by. He only knew that he needed to work. He had to stay focused even though he was finding it nearly impossible. He had to find a way to push down the memory of his sick little boy and the hurt that it caused him to feel. Every time he lost his focus and he let his thoughts slip, he began to see the images within his mind of his little boy laying in that hospital bed, and he had to push himself harder to stay focused on the task at hand.

George was hammering the metal, swinging the hammer harder and harder with every blow. He was in a deep state of concentration when he was startled by a woman's voice that came from behind him.

"George?"

George's head snapped at the sound, and he was shocked to look back and to find his wife, Melissa, standing behind him around thirty feet to the east side of the cabin.

"Liz." George said in a surprised and squeaky voice. George looked back down at his iron in the fire for a moment and then placed it, along with his tools, safely aside.

George stood up straight and turned to look quizzically at his wife as he asked, "you startled me. What's going on? What are you doing here?"

"George." Melissa said softly and gave her husband a tender smile before she continued, "nothing is going on, and everything is fine. I hope it's okay with you that I decided to come out here, and that I brought the kids out here with me. They are still in the carriage. I told them to wait there, because" Melissa let her voice fall off and she did not complete the sentence. She did not want to admit to her husband that she had told the children to wait in the carriage because she was not entirely certain of the condition that she would find George in when they reached the cabin.

"Good. That's great. I'm happy to see you." George gave his wife a relieved little smile, and he took a few small steps in her direction as he continued, "Liz, I went into town today." George stopped and stood in front of his wife and looked down at her beautiful face.

Melissa looked up at her husband with a thin smile and said, "I know. I heard that you were in town and that you looked pretty despondent while you were there. I figured that it meant that the package finally arrived." Melissa waited for a moment and knew from George's expression and his head shaking that the answer was yes.

Melissa tilted her head and asked softly, "have you looked at it yet?"

George straightened his back and stood a little taller as he spoke. "No. I have not. I don't know why I haven't. I just, haven't."

George looked down at the ground, and then turned to look across the desert brush surrounding his homestead and his cabin and noticed that all of the desert shrubs had changed and taken on gray colors with the changing of the seasons. Everything had changed so fast, and George was struggling to adjust and to cope with the changes at a time when he just wanted everything to go back to the way that it was when little George was still alive, and that it would always stay the same.

Melissa understood and nodded in agreement, and then suggested, "that's alright. Would it be okay with you if I go and get the kids into the cabin, and then maybe we can all look at it for the first time together?"

George took a moment to think about Melissa's suggestion and then decided, "yeah. That is probably the best idea. If you can get the kids together, I will go out to the cart and I'll get the crate, and then I'll bring it to the cabin. Then we can open it together."

Melissa's tone was gentle and loving when she replied, "that will be good, George. I'll go and get the kids. And when you're ready, you can get and bring the crate inside. Is that alright with you?"

Melissa was cautious and delicate in how she worded things when she spoke to her husband. There were too many times when she had been forced to stifle a scream, or she had been forced to turn and take a sudden leave in order to avoid having an emotional breakdown in public after someone had said something that had triggered such an overwhelming sense of grief that she couldn't stand it. George had been very careful about what he said and how he had said it to Melissa, and it was only fair that she made the same effort for him. Their marriage had always been based on love and mutual respect, and it was something, probably the only thing, which had not changed.

"Of course." George said flatly and looked at his wife from underneath heavy eyelids. He attempted to smile, but to Melissa, the depths of her husband's sorrow could not be more plainly obvious.

Melissa smiled delicately and then quietly turned to make her way towards the carriage. She looked down towards the ground and focused on her steps and her footing. She looked up and waved at the kids as she approached the carriage while she announced, "you can both get down from the carriage now. Your dad is out behind the cabin at his forge. He's just finishing up with some of his work and he will be out front in a moment."

Pearl and Archie both jumped out from the back of the small carriage, and their little voices climbed in competition as they debated who was going to be the first one to reach the front door. Melissa quietly told them, "kids, calm yourselves. I know that you are excited, but you have to relax. Your brothers, Robert, William, and Harry are going to be done with work soon and they will be back here anytime. As soon as they get here, we have something that we think is particularly important and very serious that we need to do. So, just relax, and then, after we are done, you can go and play with your toys."

The children grumbled, but eventually, they both agreed to do what their mother had told them. Melissa took a deep breath and asked the children to aid her by carrying a few things that she had picked up over the weeks and had remembered to bring with her on this trip. She handed an open crate to Pearl that held new, fresh washcloths, and some new kitchen items, including new cups and new flatware. She placed another crate into the arms of her son, Archie. The second crate held some clothing, some soaps that Melissa bought from the new pharmacy, a new bedroll, and some new sheets to cover and protect it, and a rolled-up newspaper that was too large for the crate and so it protruded from the top of the open crate.

Melissa picked up two water containers that she had bought new and had filled with boiled water. George had already replaced all of the water containers on the site since the recent changes in their lives had forced them to burn and replace almost everything that had been inside of the cabin. Still, Liz wanted to ensure that her husband would always have enough water on site, and so she decided to purchase and bring the new containers to him at the cabin. She carried the containers, one in each hand, and told the children, "hurry up and come along now. Let's go see your dad."

The children tried to run, but their strides were short and clumsy, and Melissa laughed at the way that the children waddled from side to side as they carried the crates. When the children reached the porch, Archie placed the box that he was carrying onto the wooden boards of the patio immediately in front of his feet, while Pearl stood a short distance behind him and gently swung her box from side to side.

Melissa placed the water containers next to the front door and brushed her hands off against her trousers. As she turned her focus towards the front door of the cabin, she suddenly realized that she was not ready to go inside of the structure. She had not been to visit the place in some time, and though she knew that George had already cleaned the place out and had burned nearly everything that was inside, she was dumbfounded by how strong the urge and the sensation to avoid the cabin actually felt. She was simply not ready to look inside of the cabin and at the space where her little boy had become so significantly ill.

Melissa felt a wave of relief when she heard the sound of horses coming from the southern road. Melissa recognized the gait of the gallop, and she immediately knew that the horses were moving fast. Melissa looked towards the road and said softly, "kids, it sounds like your brothers are coming up the trail, and since that noise is likely them, then they should arrive here in just a couple of minutes or so."

Melissa turned and looked over towards her only daughter and smiled as she said, "Pearl, you can put that crate down if you would like to."

Pearl placed the crate on the porch beside the other crate that her brother, Archie, had been carrying, and then turned to look back towards the road, and across the vast landscape. The little girl's chestnut brown hair, emerald eyes, and soft features were a striking resemblance to that of her mother. All of the children had similar features, with rich brown hair and soft hazel green eyes. The only exception had been little George, who had the faintest traces of his mother's soft copper freckles but, otherwise, with his bright blue eyes and his black hair, he had been the only child that had looked just like his father.

Robert, William, and Harry became concerned when they spotted their mother's carriage from the road below, and each one had felt a deep sense of relief when they reached the front of the cabin and found their mother and their siblings standing on the porch, where they were waiting, waving, and smiling. The boys let their horses guide them into the yard before getting them turned around and stopped near the hitching posts, where the boys dismounted their horses and tied the animals up safely.

George took his time cleaning up his workspace. He made certain that the fire was down, and although it was still smoldering, he knew that it was safe to leave it unattended. George heard the horses making their approach up the foothills and he knew that the older boys had returned after a long, hard day of work. He glanced over his workspace one last time in order to ensure that everything would be safe, and then walked around on the east side of the cabin and towards the porch and his family.

George walked around towards the front of the cabin and offered his family a warm, soft smile as he said quietly, "hey, kiddos." His brilliant blue eyes glistened in the soft golden glow of the setting sun. Pearl and Archie turned quickly, and ran towards their father, hugging him tightly around the waist.

George draped his arms around his youngest children and smiled brightly, and said through a chuckle, "well, I sure missed you guys too."

Robert, William, and Harry were further relieved when they walked up to the front of the cabin and found their father there, hugging their brother and sister. The boys sauntered towards the porch and turned their focus towards greeting their parents. They hugged their mother, and then their father, and then patted their little siblings on the tops of their heads before falling into an awkward silence.

Robert was the first to grow uncomfortable enough to break the silence by asking, "so, what's going on? The last thing that I heard Mom say about this place was that she never wanted to set foot anywhere on this property again, and that we should just burn this whole place down to the ground. That was only like a week ago. So, what's up?"

Harry could not help himself, and he gave in to the temptation. He looked at his older brother with a cunning and twisted smile and said in a questioning and teasing tone, "perhaps she is here to do it?"

William laughed uneasily at the comment. Though Melissa was harmless, William had become slightly concerned when Melissa had mentioned burning the cabin down, given that during the same conversation she had also promised that she would never wear a formal dress again, and she had taken to wearing only pantsuits, trousers, and denim jeans since that very day. If she was serious about the trousers, she might also be serious about burning the cabin down.

Robert looked over at William, and then at Harry. He shook his head from side to side. It was clear that Robert disapproved of his younger siblings' attempt at comedy.

Harry said softly, "I'm sorry. I just wanted to make everyone laugh." As he spoke, his cheeks took on a soft peach color, and then he stood upright and made a genuine effort to straighten himself up.

George did not mind the boys and their sense of humor, but it was time for George and Melissa to have a serious moment with their children. George snickered at the joke and then interrupted the boys with a booming voice, "that is very funny, boys. But your mother is not here to burn down the cabin. She brought your brother and sister out here because we had a package come in today. I picked it up from the train station this morning, and we made the decision just a little while ago that we would all open the package together."

The children looked at their father with curious expressions as he continued, "the crate is still on the cart, and I need to go and get it. The sun is setting quickly, and I think that now is probably a good time to open it."

George stepped down from the porch and made his way towards his horse, Silver, with his family watching from behind him. As he approached the horse, he felt the same deep inner conflict that he had been feeling for weeks. A mixture of panic and anxiety washed over him. He had to focus on steadying his breathing, and he had to force himself to keep going until he passed by the horse, and he was standing in front of the cart. He stood there looking directly down at the package.

As George looked down at the wooden crate, he took a deep breath, and he quietly accepted the fact that it was time to open it. He reached out slowly, and he was cautious in handling and lifting the crate. As he carefully lifted the crate, he pulled it in towards him and then held it tightly against his chest. George took several deep breaths, then turned with the crate and walked back towards the cabin.

The sunset colored the clouds with vibrant fiery reds, and it covered the ground at George's feet with a soft pink glow. George stopped in front of the porch and stood immediately in front of Melissa, and asked, "where do you think that it would be best to do this?" George looked at her with questioning, raised eyebrows.

Melissa gave George a simple little smile and said, "right here. The sun is setting, but everything looks absolutely beautiful out here right now because of the red sunset, and there is still plenty of light. Open it here so that we can see it under the last of the natural daylight."

George placed the crate at Melissa's feet, and then reached into his right, rear trouser pocket, and pulled out a small rod that had a forked end. George looked at the tool that he smithed some hours earlier in his outdoor workshop, specifically for opening the crate. George used the tool to pry at the lid on the wooden crate, and small pieces of the wood splintered off from it and broke free, falling, and landing quietly on the porch. George pried at the container again, and then again, until the top of the crate was loose enough to break free. With the top loose and ready to come off, George stopped suddenly and took a moment to simply look at the crate.

"Melissa," George said tiredly. He wanted to lift the top from the crate, and he wanted to reveal the contents of the package, but he did not know if he had the strength inside of his soul to do it.

"The top is ready to come off. Can you, please? Just take the top off, please." George asked, and then stood up slowly. He looked down at his wife, and his heart broke.

Melissa recognized the look on George's face. He had never been the soft, or the emotional type. But she did know when the emotions were running high, and when he needed some help to get through things. Melissa nodded her head yes, took a deep breath, and remained silent. She crouched down in front of the crate and made herself comfortable in the position. When she was balanced and steady in her crouched position, she carefully reached out, gently removed the top from the box, and exposed a layer of soft, black velvety paper. She placed the top beside the box and then reached into the box and pulled back the soft velvet-like paper.

Inside of the box was the most beautifully cut blue-gray granite stone that both George and Melissa had ever seen. It had taken several weeks for it to arrive, and it had been incredibly expensive to have it made. The twelve-inch wide, by fourteen inch tall, by four inch thick, cut stone had a perfectly rounded top, and there were beautiful, delicate leaves on short vines engraved into the face that lined the rounded top. The inscription below the leaves read, George Graham Henderson. Born Dec. 15, 1890. Died Sept. 14, 1899.

Melissa took a deep breath and then stammered as she began to sob, "it is absolutely perfect. I can't believe that he's gone."

George looked at the perfect stone and broke down in tears too. The children all gathered around, and they put as many arms around their parents as they could. They were all heartbroken over losing little George. He was the one that had brought his mother flowers whenever she was sick. He was the one that sat with his older siblings and would read to them when they were having a dreadful day. He was the one that thought about other people and was always excited about being a part of something that was bigger than himself. Losing little George meant that they had all essentially lost a very important piece of themselves.

After a little time, Melissa looked down through her teary eyes at the headstone and said in a disappointed and deeply bitter tone, "I suppose that we will need to take this into the city tomorrow." She wiped her face hastily with the back of her hands, and then she tried to compose herself.

George pulled out his handkerchief and offered it to Melissa. She waved it off and declined to take it from him, and so he used it to wipe his face. It was hard for George to see the older boys break down, and as their father, he did his best to put himself back together. He looked at his children, their eyes still wet from tears.

George thought about it for a moment, and as he slipped the handkerchief back into his trouser pocket he stated, "unfortunately, we cannot take it tomorrow. I have to work, and the boys also have to work tomorrow. And I need to make some arrangements with the cemetery in order to have it placed. In reality, it's going to take a few days, maybe even a couple of weeks to have it placed. But, Liz, there is something else that I think needs to be considered, because the way that I see it is this: we don't have to do anything. We can take it into the city when we have some free time, and we don't need to be in any kind of a hurry to get it there because the stone is ours, we paid for it, and we can do whatever we want with it."

Melissa let out a long sigh and said flatly, "the base is already installed, George. They are already expecting to have the stone placed in the cemetery."

George nodded his head in agreement and said, "sure. But there are a few things that are weighing on me right now. First, this is actually not what we ordered. It is such a beautiful stone that I hate to point out that they made a mistake, but the name is incomplete. It should read George Graham Henderson, Jr. Unfortunately, it will likely take a few months to get a new stone made with the correct name, and I am betting that I am going to have to spend another small fortune to have it made."

George let out a little sigh, took a quick breath and continued, "second, we are pretty well-known in this county. But the cemetery is on the outskirts of the city and it is in a fairly rural area. If people should happen to notice his headstone with my name in that cemetery, anything could happen to it. It could be vandalized or stolen. Perhaps even worse would be if the cemetery should become neglected or fall into disrepair. You know that this concept of placing everyone from every station in life, with the good beside the bad all in one Cemetery, is very progressive. They have had a couple of problems already, and what is basically my name could become lost there in that field."

Melissa let out a loud scoff and said sharply, "George, if you were so worried about all of that, then why didn't we have him buried somewhere else?"

Robert dried his eyes on his sleeve. His face and his cheeks were streaked with dirt and tears. He stifled his sobs and said, "Mom, Dad, I think that I need to say something."

Robert choked on his words and struggled to find his voice. He took a few short and shallow breaths and then focused on getting the right words to come out and said, "I think you're both focusing on the wrong things. Georgie loved it here. This is where he lived, and, yeah, this is also where he got sick. Unfortunately, it's also pretty much where he died. Sure, he went to the hospital, and then to the cemetery. But this," Robert pointed down towards the ground beneath his feet. The small veins along Robert's forehead popped out as he continued emphatically, "this is where it happened. This is where it all happened! And everything that happened, it happened here because this is where Georgie wanted to be. And this is where he wanted to be because he loved it here, and there was nothing that you or anybody else could have done to convince him to stay home and to stay away from this place."

Robert's voice cracked as he spoke, and his deeply reddened eyes flooded with tears. He blinked back at the heavy tears and then said softly, "honestly, I think you should just place it here. You're arguing over small details that in reality, they don't even matter. Forget about taking it all that way into the city. This is his stone, and it's beautiful. And I think that this is where you should place it."

George looked over at Melissa, and it was obvious to him that she was heavily contemplating the idea. George raised his eyebrows in high arches as he thought about the idea and then said to Melissa, "you know, that really is not such a bad idea. Robert is right. Georgie absolutely loved it here from the very first moment that he saw it. And this place is ours. The cabin isn't perfect, but our claim on it as a homestead is still fairly new, and I really don't think that we have any plans on selling it anytime soon. If we keep the stone here, it will allow us to visit him, sort of, anytime that we want."

Melissa swallowed hard and stated with a scared, and empty voice, "it's just that we are supposed to take it into the city. But I suppose that some people would change their minds about this sort of thing if given the opportunity. Since we have the opportunity, and since this is the last thing that we are ever really going to buy for him, I don't want to let it go. However, I also don't want my son to be left alone in an unmarked grave. So whatever we do, wherever it is that we put it, we all have to agree to it. There are no right or wrong answers, and there is only deciding where to place it. Right?"

The children broke out into a clamor, their voices overlapping, all in agreement and all suggesting that they should place the beautiful headstone in the place where the little boy had his play space, next to the hole where he loved to dig and look for Gold. George looked down at his family as they debated the solution, and he was suddenly overcome with so much appreciation and love for his little family unit that amongst the noise he was beginning to feel whole and human again.

"Ok, so it's decided." Melissa announced very suddenly.

Melissa felt the hot tears in her eyes rising again and tried without success to blink them away. She realized that the tears were unavoidable, and she pointed west and did her best to speak clearly, "George, if it's alright with you and if you should agree, according to the children we should place the headstone over there on the west side of the cabin beside the troughs and nearby the hole where Georgie loved to dig and play."

George blinked back at the fresh tears that were forming in his eyes and asked with a thick and heavy tongue, "everybody agrees?"

He was answered with solid yesses from all of the members of his family. Pearl added her opinion by emphasizing, "I agree. You should get a different one for the cemetery if you really want to. But this stone should go right over there where Georgie liked to play, and I know that it's the right thing to do because I don't think that we've all ever agreed on anything more, Daddy."

George smiled at his little girl, and then carefully removed the heavy stone from the crate and pulled it in closely against him. It was awkward and heavy, but it did not matter. George held the stone so tightly against his chest that it appeared to be nearly weightless in his arms. He took small steps over to where his little boy had played and looked for gold during the long, scorching summer.

With his family immediately behind him, George looked down at the hole that little George had been so diligently working on, and he made a silent promise to his little boy that he would continue digging and would look for gold. George scanned the ground, and beside the old trough, he found a large boulder with a squared face that would make a perfect easel for the beautiful headstone. George knelt down slowly and placed the headstone onto the ground facing east, leaning it gently against the square boulder beside the trough. George stayed in the crouched position for a moment as he gazed upon the stone, and then he stood up and turned to look at his wife.

The tears flowed freely from Melissa's eyes, and she looked down at the stone and said out loud, "I love you, son. I'm so sorry that this happened to you." She sobbed and turned to her husband, who reached out, took her into his arms, and pulled her against him.

The children all gathered around, crouching, and squatting down to get a closer look at the stone under the last of the sun's soft pink daylight. Melissa calmed herself, turned her face and pressed her cheek against her husband's chest and looked down at her children under the soft glow from the sunset and let out a long, deep sigh. As the last glimmer of the sun disappeared somewhere into the depths of darkness behind the Bradshaw Mountains along the western horizon, Melissa said tenderly, "at least if it's here, then he will not ever be forgotten about."

Chapter 19

February 2020 - Dewey, Arizona

The warmth from the afternoon sun was a relief on that cool winter day. Jennifer looked around the property and carefully examined the area where the headstone had been located. She was already prepared to humor the officer before she arrived. "Sir, I looked through all of the records, and I put it all together. There were no permits, and there are no records for a gravesite here, and that is because there isn't one."

The officer took notes and looked up to watch her inquisitively as Jennifer explained and summarized why the headstone was found in the wash, along with details pertaining to what happened to the little boy.

"The little boy died in 1899, from typhoid. He was buried in Prescott, in the Citizen's Cemetery, and his family memorialized his death here because this is where he was when he fell ill, and it is where the death truly occurred. Back then when they placed this stone here, Arizona wasn't officially a part of the federal union yet. The town of Dewey didn't even really exist, and this area was simply referred to as the Lynx Creek district back then. The headstone and the records are simply that old, and I needed to search for them in a historical context. It was rather challenging to find them."

Jennifer took a sharp, deep breath and continued, "it is unfortunate, but the records indicate that the Henderson family endured a lot of hardships. The boy's father, George Sr., he was working at the then-new power plant in Walker, in 1913, when he was killed in a terrible and tragic electrical accident. Then the little boy's oldest brother, Robert, died suddenly and tragically in 1915. Sometime shortly after that, the boy's only sister Pearl, and her husband, went through a divorce. A few years after that, the little boy's mother, Melissa, moved with her daughter, Pearl, and Pearl's children, out to a big coastal city in Southern California. It's really unfortunate, and I don't believe for a moment that they intended it, but it seems to me like they went through so many challenges over time that they forgot about the headstone. Nobody ever did find any gold on this property, and then the father died, the brother died, and then the mother and the sister moved to a different state, and as such, all of the evidence that exists suggests that they simply forgot that the headstone was still here."

Jennifer stopped for a moment and then crouched down over a small hole that she noticed on the slope of the hill. The officer watched as she reached down and flicked a few small stones from the shallow hole, and then her slender fingers coiled up tightly into a fist. Jennifer stood up quickly and held out her hand, and then she quickly turned her hand over and opened it with her palm facing upward, revealing the antique, hand-wrought, rusty, iron nail that she had retrieved from the dirt.

As she held out the old and rusty artifact for the officer to see for himself, she continued, "the Henderson family had a homestead claim and a miners shack here, hence these old, antique nails in the dirt. This area in particular was cleared out of all of the dilapidated miners' shacks sometime in the 1960's. A few of the shacks that were in the area and were still in decent condition, those buildings were all sold off and moved to other places. But whatever was dilapidated and was too far gone and could not be moved and sold, those were all burned to the ground and then the entire site was dozed over and cleared."

Jennifer used her hand and the antique nail to gesture and to point towards the house and the driveway that were behind her, and then stated, "if you look at the grade of the existing building pad, everything that was here before this house was erected, it was all burned out and then cleared by pushing everything into the wash that is right in front of here where we are standing. Burned wood, the old nails, any garbage that might have been laying around, everything that was here was pushed into this wash, and it all wound up buried right here under a few feet of dirt. Unfortunately, this included the headstone.

The headstone was pushed into this washed-out area with the rest of the burned-up garbage."

The officer tapped the back end of his ballpoint pen against the small notebook that he held with his left hand, and then turned the pen around and used it to make a quick note. He thought about what Jennifer had said for a moment and then asked, "do you think that they knew about the headstone when they cleared the building site to build this house?"

Jennifer smiled at the officer, and replied, "your guess is as good as mine. It is hard to say what they knew, or who might have known about it. It is possible that the desert brush had grown tall around the stone since these shrubs can reach heights that exceed ten feet tall. It may have been covered up and hidden under a mess of foliage and debris, and as such it may not have been observed by the work crew that burned and cleared the site. It is also possible that they found the headstone and that they intentionally pushed it into the wash because it might have affected their ability to continue to work. Let's face it- finding a headstone on a construction site is the equivalent of a stop-work order, and not everybody is honest."

The officer snickered playfully and in agreement with the comment, and Jennifer continued, "I don't know what they knew, and I don't think that there is any way to find out or to prove it. It's just falling into one of those periods or eras where there isn't a lot of documentation available, and there's just no way to know what they might have known about it back then."

The officer smiled in amusement and said, "that's probably right. I just thought that I would ask since you found a lot of information that pertains to the headstone. I mean, you found information that I couldn't even find. Would you email me the information that you just gave to me so that I can add that information to my report? I'll give you my card, and I'll print my email address on the back of it." The officer took out his wallet and pulled out a business card, quickly scribbled his email address onto the back of it, and then handed it to Jennifer.

Jennifer took the business card, smiled, and said, "of course. I can have that information to you before the end of the workday. No problem."

The officer smiled warmly back at Jennifer, and said, "thank you for taking the time to research this, because I really couldn't find any of the records, and that would have drastically changed the situation that your company is up against. It is unusual, and I honestly haven't heard of anyone else ever taking a call like this. It's pretty incredible to find a piece of history like this literally sitting in someone's backyard."

Jennifer nodded in agreement with the officer. It was incredible. Except, it also created a new problem that needed to be dealt with, and she decided to ask the sheriff about it.

Jennifer smiled shyly and said, "hey, before you go, there is one thing that is bothering me, and I don't know what to do about it." In a comical tone, Jennifer continued, "you see, we found this historical headstone, and now that I have it, I don't know what to do with it because the cemetery that it belongs to has been closed for nearly a century. Should I take it and place it on the gravesite? Or is that illegal? Do I need special permission or a permit to place it in the cemetery?"

The officer stifled a small chuckle and attempted to maintain his professionalism as he explained, "from what I know, that cemetery is a registered historical site, and as you just stated it hasn't been active for a very long time. I think that it might be best if you tried contacting a local business that works with headstones. They might be able to assist you with getting it placed. Also, you should probably try getting in touch with someone down at the county. There should be someone down there that will be able to advise you on what you can and cannot do within the cemetery."

Jennifer smiled thankfully as she replied, "I'll try that when I get back to the office. I'll take a look at the website for the county, and hopefully, I can get the headstone placed where it rightfully belongs. Thank you so much for all of your help and for your time."

"You're welcome." The officer said as he smiled back at her.

When the officer was assured that there was nothing else that was needed for his report, he said goodbye to Jennifer and left in his white-marked SUV.

As soon as the officer was gone, Jennifer said goodbye to Mark, and then hurried back to her black Cadillac. Before she could get the car started, she was already carefully planning the details that she wanted to include in the email that she planned to send to the officer, and to the county.

Chapter 20
April 20, 2021 - Prescott, Arizona

Jennifer sent a lengthy email to Yavapai County explaining everything that she had learned about the headstone and the Henderson family. It took a little more than a year to finalize all of the details, but the representatives at Yavapai County were astounded by what occurred with the headstone, and with what happened to the little boy, and they agreed to place the headstone on the child's gravesite in the Prescott Citizen's Cemetery.

Jennifer arrived at the cemetery early that afternoon. Seeing that she was alone, she took a longer time than she usually would to smooth out her black slacks and her pin striped button up shirt, and then she waited to see if anyone else was going to show up. She was anxious, but there was an easiness to her as she anticipated the days events.

She did not have to wait alone for very long. A taxi arrived and dropped off a local historian, and within a minute the cars began to flow into the cemetery, nearly filling a section of it with people that were interested in seeing the headstone. Jennifer watched as more and more people joined the group. She listened to the discussions that were casually taking place, and it provided her with a reminder of how important the cemetery was, and still is.

The Citizen's Cemetery opened in 1864 and closed in 1933, and it is listed in the National Register of Historical places. The cemetery was intended to be an affordable final resting place for everyone regardless of their position in life, with the cost for each plot starting at $2.50, and not more than $99. The old were buried beside the very young, the poor were buried beside the wealthy, and the good were buried beside the bad. It was truly a final resting place for all. The cemetery is unique from a historical context because every person that was interred in the cemetery was an early pioneer in the county and played a significant role in the early development of the area and contributed to the growth of the region. They were all early pioneers of Yavapai County, and they endured and survived unbelievably difficult and harsh conditions so that our towns would survive and would continue to exist today. The life of a pioneer was not easy, and out of the three thousand burials that took place in this cemetery, fewer than one thousand of its gravesites have headstones.

Jennifer listened to the many discussions that were taking place, and as she looked across the group, she smiled. They were all there to see the little boy's headstone, and they were all eagerly waiting to see it placed at the head of his grave site. After all this time, it was incredible to see the large number of people that showed up to honor the life of the little boy whose gravesite had no markers, and whose identity had nearly become lost in time.

After 88 years of closure, the Citizens Cemetery was opened to the public for a memorial service for little George Henderson. Included in attendance were representatives of the Governor of the state of Arizona, elected representatives from Yavapai County District 1 and Yavapai County District 2, other representatives from Yavapai County, historians, and many other interested citizens.

As the service began, Jennifer looked across the field of old graves that were covered with wildflowers and were blooming with vibrant colors of fuchsia, amethyst, and indigo, and she smiled brightly. With the sun shining overhead, and with the smell of fresh spring blossoms flooding the air, the group gathered and watched on as representatives of Yavapai County placed the headstone for Little George Graham Henderson, Jr. at his gravesite.

After 121 years, George Graham Henderson, Jr. is in a marked grave in the Citizen's Cemetery, in Prescott, Arizona.

"Mr. and Mrs. G. G. Henderson of Lynx Creek, desire the Journal Miner to thank neighbors and friends for the many acts of kindness during the recent illness and subsequently the death of their little son.

Geo. Henderson, son of Mr. and Mrs. G. G. Henderson, of Lynx Creek died last week of typhoid fever. Deceased was 8 years old and was an unusually bright boy, and a great favorite with all who knew him."

(Arizona Weekly Journal-Miner, 1899).

The End.

A fterword

The records indicate that George Henderson Sr., immigrated from Quebec, Canada, to Arizona sometime around the year 1876. His name first appears in newspapers in the Yavapai County region sometime around the year of 1892, when he was elected and appointed as an election officer and as a mine inspector in Lynx Creek. His name appears on a number of county surveys requesting that the county record and register a number of different mines and mineral lodes throughout the territory of Yavapai County. During that same year it was also reported that George held a seat at the republican convention. In reality, George must have already become involved in politics in Prescott and in Yavapai County at an earlier time than was previously suggested.

George and Melissa were married in 1883. It was stated in Melissa's obituary that she was born and married in Canada, though there were no other official records available that might have been used to verify this. There are no vital/official records to directly indicate where they were living when they decided to get married. There are some sporadic reports and records which suggest that one or more of Melissa's brothers either resided in, or frequently traveled to visit the Prescott region between the early 1880's and the late 1890's.

George prospered in Yavapai County as a politician. He became the Walker district school superintendent, a deputy, a justice of the peace for Yavapai County, a representative and elected official of Yavapai County, while he continued to grow his family businesses in ranching, transportation, lodging, and mining. George and Melissa must have become quite successful, as the newspapers throughout the next decade of their lives frequently reported that the couple was seen visiting the city or that they were in the city for a number of days on a business trip, and that they were registered to stay in some of Prescott's most luxurious hotels. Furthermore, in 1902, a new passenger train line became available. It was a daily express line that traveled non-stop from

Lynx Creek directly to Prescott. The proprietor of that direct express line was Mr. G. G. Henderson.

Though there are a lot of records to indicate that George was successful in most of his endeavors, there are other records which indicate that their lives as early pioneers were not any easier because of it. While George was really great at his job, which was what made him successful, it also meant that he would become directly involved with the transport of some of his friends after they had been in truly terrible accidents. It was one thing to move livestock across the state by railroad, and it was quite another thing to use horses to transport people that he was personally associated with who were crushed or were otherwise injured by the mining accidents, some of which were so severely injured that they were ultimately going to lose their lives. It wouldn't have been easy. His work would have been mentally and emotionally challenging, and there were times in which it would have been downright dangerous.

George registered several mines throughout the county, some of which he collected and held in his own asset portfolio, and others which he sold off to other people or to businesses along the way. There was a specific mining claim that George registered that is of particular interest. The old mining claim was located in Walker, and George sold that claim and that property to the Arizona power company. The Arizona power company converted the old claim and used the property to build a new power substation. In July of 1913, George was working as a superintendent at that power substation on the property that he had previously sold to the Arizona Power Company. It was reported that George was replacing an iron bedstead from one of the towers at the substation, and that he was unaware that the electrical wires around him were live.

Witnesses said that George placed his right hand on one of the live wires, and as soon as his other hand and his hammer came into contact with the iron bedstead, there was an immediate flash and an explosion, at which time George's entire body ignited and caught on fire. The reports indicate that his whole head was significantly burned, and that his neck, chest, arms, and one of his legs down to his ankle, were all severely burned. The witnesses to the horrific accident said that George remained conscious throughout the entirety of the event even though he was so significantly burned that on some places of his skull the lacerations revealed bone, and his features were unrecognizable. He was taken to the Sisters of Mercy Hospital where he unfortunately succumbed to his injuries some hours later on the same day.

Melissa had her husband buried in the Mountain View Cemetery, in Prescott. There is no documentation or no records that exist which might be used to determine why Melissa had her husband interred at the Mountain View cemetery rather than the Citizens Cemetery with their little son. However, the records do indicate that Melissa continued to be a favorite in the city of Prescott, and over time the newspapers made frequent reports that the Walker resident was seen visiting the city. The one thing that is constant throughout the records is that Melissa was generally at the center of the suffering that occurred as a result of the tragic events that occurred in their family.

Melissa's misfortune would continue, and in November of 1915, Robert, who was her second child and her oldest son, and was said to be suffering from ill health for some time, died as a result of a self-inflicted gunshot wound. The reports around the time of the unfortunate event indicate that Robert had been suffering from appendicitis and had only recently returned to his home in Mayer, a neighboring town of Lynx Creek, after an extended trip to California where he was visiting and was searching for solutions for his failing health. The records indicate that Robert was married at the time of his death, however, he did not have any children.

Just a few months later in March of 1916, Archie, and William, discovered an eighteen-inch-wide vein of gold running through one of their Walker mining claims. The discovery created a lot of excitement throughout the mining community, and the brothers used that new gold fortune to expand and to acquire additional gold and silver mines, and it allowed the family to buy out a number of homesteads within the region. There were also reports to indicate that Harry, and William, went on to successfully develop the family's ranching business and that they experienced excellent performance in the cattle business. It was reported that Harry was an excellent cattleman, and he was well-known as a championship bronco rider in the Prescott Frontier Days rodeo contests.

In 1917, the brothers Harry, and William, who were actually twins and were born in Prescott, and their youngest brother Archie, were called by the government through a draft to report for military duty. The locals all agreed that it was particularly coincidental that all three of the brothers should be called up for the draft given the fact that the brothers were literally the only three eligible persons to register for the draft from that entire region. Based on the newspaper reports, the draft was a striking blow to the Henderson family. It meant that Melissa, who had already lost two of her sons, George, and Robert, could perhaps lose all three of her surviving sons to the same war. The records indicate that the brothers were stationed in Germany for an unknown period of time, with William having been stationed in Germany for several years as a result of the draft. In 1922, the newspapers suggested that all of the Henderson boys had finally returned home from the war, and they were registered for the Frontier-Day's lineup, an event for which they had been prominent contestants.

Melissa continued to be a prominent figure in Prescott, and a favorite in pioneer circles. The reports indicate that she remained in the Walker area until sometime around the year 1924, after which time she moved to a larger city in southern California with her daughter, Pearl. The records indicate that the mother and daughter lived together, and they took on work as commercial seamstresses.

Between the mid 1920's and the early 1930's, the newspapers shifted focus and there were fewer reports pertaining to the Henderson family during and following this period of time, and there are only a few small details that are known about their family from that point forward. It appears from those reports as though the Henderson boys continued to experience success in farming, ranching, and mining.

In September of 1931, the newspapers reported that William, died as a result of a self-inflicted gunshot wound at his home which shared the same address and location as his wife's business, the Busy Bee Restaurant, in Prescott. The reports indicate that William and his wife were experiencing marital problems, and also that heavy drinking may have been involved with the incident. The newspapers were unaware or failed to make the connection that William turned the gun on himself on September 13th, 1931, and that the self-destructive event actually occurred on the evening of the anniversary of his little brother George's death. William did not have any children.

In October of 1934, the newspapers reported that Melissa died in the home of her only daughter, Pearl. Though the reports claimed that Melissa was expected to be buried in Southern California, her remains were brought back to Prescott, where she was interred at the Mountain View Cemetery. Melissa's obituary stated that she was survived by her daughter, Pearl, and by her two sons, Harry, and Archie, of Dewey. Melissa was known as Mrs. G. G. Henderson until the day that she died.

Harry continued to reside in Lynx Creek, later called Dewey, and he continued to work as a rancher throughout the Prescott, Walker, Dewey, and Mayer areas. In some of the records his name was incorrectly listed or recorded as either Henry or Perry. The records indicate that Harry continued to be a championship bronco rider for several years, and that he experienced great success in cattle ranching. Harry was married at the time of his death. However, he did not have any children. Harry died in December of 1952, as a result of heart disease.

Archie continued working as a miner, and as a rancher at his family's farm in Walker. Archie was well-known in the region, and it was reported that his mining production was substantial and successful. The newspaper reports suggest that Archie may have become involved in politics as well. Archie was married, and he had at least five children. Archie died in August of 1953, after several years of living with rheumatic endocarditis (an infection in the heart).

The records indicate that Pearl stayed in her southern California home after Melissa's passing. Pearl was actually the oldest of all of the Henderson children. As was previously suggested, Pearl was married and later divorced, and from that marriage she had at least two children. In October of 1953, only two months after her brother Archie passed, the newspapers reported that Pearl had also died. The final records for Pearl (and for the Henderson family) indicate that she was cremated, and that all of her final services (clergymen, cemetery, flowers) were to be handled privately by her family. The exact location of Pearl's burial site is unknown.

George Graham Henderson, Sr., Born in 1846. Died on Jul 8, 1913. He was 67 years old. George was buried in the Mountain View Cemetery, in Prescott.

Robert J. Henderson. Born January 31, 1886. Died on November 4, 1915. He was 29 years old. Robert was buried in the Mountain View Cemetery in Prescott, beside his father.

William Willis Henderson. Born July 6, 1888. Died on September 13, 1931. He was 43 years old. William was buried in the Mountain View Cemetery in Prescott, beside his father and his brother, Robert.

Malicie "Melissa" Elizabeth Richards Henderson. Born November 9, 1851. Died on October 31, 1934. She was 82 years old. Melissa was buried in the Mountain View Cemetery in Prescott, beside her husband and her sons, Robert, and William.

Harry W. Henderson. Born July 6, 1888. Died on December 21, 1952. He was 64 years old. Harry was buried in the Mountain View Cemetery in Prescott, beside his father and his mother, and his two brothers, Robert, and William.

Archie Richard Henderson. Born July 31, 1893. Died on August 18, 1953. He was 60 years old. Archie was buried in the Mountain View Cemetery in Prescott, beside his father, George, his mother, Malicie "Melissa," and his three brothers, Robert, William, and Harry.

Pearl May Henderson (Doan). Born March 19, 1884. Died on October 22, 1953. She was 69 years old. The public records indicate that Pearl was cremated in California. Her burial site is unknown.

Author's Note

This book is based on a true story. The author made every effort to maintain and preserve the integrity of the early pioneers and attempted to represent and recreate the people, places, events, experiences, the history, and/or other details as accurately as possible. The story was written to reflect the real conditions, real circumstances, and the real events that occurred, and it describes what most likely occurred based on the public and historical records that are available. Some of the names, events, dates, timelines, or details, may not be correct, or may have been changed in order to protect the privacy of the living.

References

Arizona Department of Health Services. (2020). Vital records. Retrieved from https://www.azdhs.gov/licensing/vital-records/genealogy/index.php

Arizona Weekly Journal-Miner. (September 13, 1899). September 13, 1899, Image 3. Prescott, Az. Retrieved from https://chroniclingamerica.loc.gov/lccn/sn85032938/1899-09-13/ed-1/seq-3/

Find a grave, database and images. (2021). Memorial page for George Graham Henderson Jr. (15 Dec 1890–14 Sep 1899), Find a Grave Memorial ID 226294531, Citizens Cemetery, Prescott, Yavapai County, Arizona, USA; Maintained by Jennifer Anger-Baeta (contributor 47915827). Retrieved from https://www.findagrave.com/memorial/226294531/george-graham-henderson

Maps of the day. (2016). Maps of the day: Travel times from NYC in 1800, 1830, 1857 and 1930. American Enterprise Institute. Retrieved from https://www.aei.org/carpe-diem/maps-of-the-day-travel-times-from-nyc-in-1800-1830-1857-and-1930/

Mountain View Cemetery. (2021). Mountain View Cemetery, Burial Index. Genealogy Trails History Group, Arizona Trails, Yavapai County. Retrieved from

http://genealogytrails.com/ariz/yavapai/cemeteries/
mountainview04.html

Yavapai County. (2020). Citizens Cemetery, Burial Index, Prescott, Arizona. Yavapai County. Retrieved from https://yavapaiaz.gov/Portals/22/BurialIndex.pdf

Don't miss out!

Visit the website below and you can sign up to receive emails whenever Jennifer D. Anger-Baeta publishes a new book. There's no charge and no obligation.

https://books2read.com/r/B-A-BQWW-JSLFC

BOOKS2READ

Connecting independent readers to independent writers.

About the Author

Jennifer was columnist for a newspaper in San Francisco before she moved away from the news desk and transitioned into an academic research position around the year 2010. She has also worked as a teacher, an editor, an independent business consultant, and a project manager.

Jennifer lives in the mountains of Arizona with her family and her children on their small farm along with her six rescued dogs, twenty-eight chickens, two ducks, one guinea pig, and one cat. Jennifer grew up in California, and after suffering head trauma in a serious motorcycle accident in 2006, she relocated to Yavapai County, Arizona.

Jennifer's formal studies were focused on forensic psychology, business management, and economics, and she completed her post graduate studies in 2018. Jennifer also studied history, and genealogy, and hopes that her writing will give her readers a true taste of Arizona, and what the wild west was really like.